Cambridge I

Elements in Ancient Egypt in Context
edited by
Gianluca Miniaci
University of Pisa
Juan Carlos Moreno García
CNRS, Paris
Anna Stevens
University of Cambridge and Monash University

THE NILE

Mobility and Management

Judith Bunbury
University of Cambridge

Reim Rowe
Independent Scholar

CAMBRIDGE
UNIVERSITY PRESS

CAMBRIDGE
UNIVERSITY PRESS

University Printing House, Cambridge CB2 8BS, United Kingdom

One Liberty Plaza, 20th Floor, New York, NY 10006, USA

477 Williamstown Road, Port Melbourne, VIC 3207, Australia

314–321, 3rd Floor, Plot 3, Splendor Forum, Jasola District Centre,
New Delhi – 110025, India

103 Penang Road, #05–06/07, Visioncrest Commercial, Singapore 238467

Cambridge University Press is part of the University of Cambridge.

It furthers the University's mission by disseminating knowledge in the pursuit of
education, learning, and research at the highest international levels of excellence.

www.cambridge.org
Information on this title: www.cambridge.org/9781108826488
DOI: 10.1017/9781108919913

© Judith Bunbury and Reim Rowe 2021

First published 2021

A catalogue record for this publication is available from the British Library.

ISBN 978-1-108-82648-8 Paperback
ISSN 2516-4813 (online)
ISSN 2516-4805 (print)

Additional resources for this publication at www.cambridge.org/bunburyrowe

The Nile

Mobility and Management

Elements in Ancient Egypt in Context

DOI: 10.1017/9781108919913
First published online: July 2021

Judith Bunbury
University of Cambridge

Reim Rowe
Independent Scholar

Author for correspondence: Judith Bunbury, jmb21@cam.ac.uk

Abstract: The ancient Egyptian kingdoms, at their greatest extent, stretched more than 2,000 kilometres along the Nile and passed through diverse habitats. In the north, the Nile traversed the Mediterranean coast and the Delta while further south a thread of cultivation along the Nile Valley passed through the vast desert of the Sahara. As global climate and landscapes changed and evolved, the habitable parts of the kingdoms shifted. Modern studies suggest that episodes of desertification and greening swept across Egypt over periods of 1,000 years. Rather than isolated events, the changes in Egypt are presented in context, often as responses to global occurrences, characterised by a constant shift of events, so although broadly historic, this narrative follows a series of habitats as they change and evolve through time.

Supplementary video available at www.cambridge.org/bunburyrowe

Keywords: Nile, ancient Egypt, river, migration, hydraulic-engineering

ISBNs: 9781108826488 (PB), 9781108919913 (OC)
ISSNs: 2516-4813 (online), 2516-4805 (print)

Contents

1 Introduction

The ancient Egyptian kingdoms, at their greatest extent, stretched more than 2,000 kilometres along the Nile and passed through diverse habitats (Figure 1). In the north, the Nile traversed the Mediterranean coast and the Delta while further south a thread of cultivation along the Nile Valley passed through the vast desert of the Sahara. As global climate and landscapes changed and evolved, the habitable parts of the kingdoms shifted. Modern studies suggest that episodes of desertification and greening swept across Egypt over periods of 1,000 years. In order to present a narrative of landscape and climate change in Egypt, we have explored the changes to the Nile Valley along with its fringing wadis and the Northern Delta.

It is also paramount to understand the human context in which these long-term climate trends occurred. With climate and landscape change as a backdrop, we explore the geo-political fortunes of Ancient Egypt as they waxed and waned through the centuries from the rather inhospitable conditions of the Nile in the wet phase of the Holocene to the population adaptions identified during cooler, arid times as sand from desert encroachment changed the Nile environment forever.

The thread that runs through this Element remains the Nile and its valley but the key theme of the Element is without doubt human. Past and current research and thinking are brought together to give a chronological timeline of the landscape of the Nile Valley, using what has been learnt from the geological history of the area and what has been discovered of ancient communities that once called the Nile their home. At its heart, this Element is also a history of geo-archaeology in Egypt, charting the development of methodologies and the key research projects that have helped shape our understanding of the Nile Valley and will continue to do so for years to come.

This Element is a dedication to the early resilience and resourcefulness of ancient Egyptians and to those who have devoted their time to understanding the Nile and her landscape.

2 Humans and Climate Change

Egypt, part of the cradle of civilisation, is a product of the Nile, the world's longest river. Since the majority of the country is desert, its people live mainly along the Nile on the fertile floodplain and delta of the river. For millennia, the population of Egypt has been subject to the river's behaviour and geography and has evolved largely in response to this great waterway. Ever since hominids in the early prehistoric period first radiated from the Rift Valley along the Nile Valley and Saharan region, the area has developed and been recognised

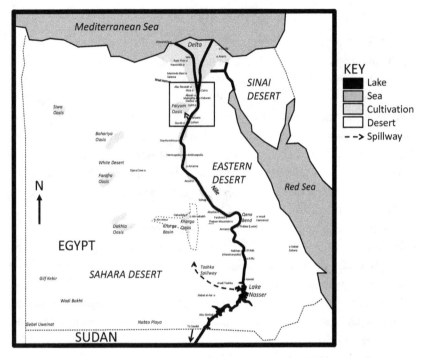

Figure 1 Map of the main places mentioned in the text.

alternatively as an important route out of Africa, a home to one of the greatest civilisations the Earth has known, and one of the most continuously inhabited and historically important tracts of land.

To give a flavour of the persistence of habitation in this area, we need to consider the time before the last ice age, around 30,000 BC, when permanent populations were already present in Egypt. Evidence remains of extensive deposits of stone tools and workshops around the Faiyum and Kharga oases. We know from redeposited tools that they also made use of habitats in the Nile Valley but subsequent river activity has destroyed traces of this period of human history.

During the glaciations of the last ice age (around 110,000 to 9640 BC), as global temperatures dropped, the Sahara became arid and inhospitable. At the same time, the Nile shrank and became more approachable as its water supply from the annual Ethiopian monsoon dwindled. At the north and south poles, cooler temperatures meant that water was locked away in the ice caps lowering global sea level and consequently reducing the water level in the Mediterranean. The Nile, eroding down to the new sea level, formed narrow canyons shrinking the habitable area of Egypt considerably.

These glacial processes were reversed during the interglacial periods, with rising temperatures causing the reinvigoration of the Ethiopian monsoon.

They also caused melting of the ice caps and hence rising sea level. The delta was flooded as the sea rose and fresh water was held back in the Nile Valley which became wet and marshy. These marshes, liable to flooding and inhabited by hippos and other large mammals, were a rich, if dangerous, habitat. Upstream, the rising Nile also extended its floodplain and, in places, overflowed into the Sahara creating a patchwork of lakes that formed an almost perfect habitat for early humans and ushered in the Holocene, the time since around 11,000 years ago. In the lake-shore environments there was access to fresh water, fish, game and, as lakes receded during dryer times, calorie-rich grains.

Throughout history, climate oscillations caused the Nile to rise and fall as well as periodically drying and rewetting the Nile margins and the Saharan lakebeds. In the wetter times, the Nile, as all rivers do, responded to the rise by rebuilding its delta and floodplain and developing into a meandering river. As the meandering river matured, the inhabitants of Egypt became increasingly dependent upon the Nile as the deserts dried. They left the deserts and migrated into the oases and to the Nile Valley flanks. With time, the Nile coalesced into fewer channels and humans came even closer to the river.

No finer example exists of the effect of climate events on the human collective psyche than the experiences of those who lived through the chaos of the First Intermediate Period (FIP). The damage caused can be seen in the Famine Stela, thought to be Ptolemaic, written about the chaos of this time when Egypt was adapting to the sudden reduction of rainfall and the lower Nile waters: "All Upper Egypt is dying of hunger ... everyone ate his children one after the other ... they have begun to eat people here ... The river of Egypt is dry and men cross the water on foot ... The place of water has become a riverbank" (Lichtheim 2006).

Closer proximity meant that the Nile dwellers began to understand how the Nile swelled and diminished through its annual cycle and also how the channels and islands behaved over the generations. This emerging knowledge was captured in myths, ceremonies and agricultural practices as well as the more empirical calendars and Nilometer records. These developments were particularly common as they were directed towards the collection of taxes. With growing expertise, an increasing number of practices designed to manage and control the Nile flood developed and accreted. In modern times, with the construction of the Aswan Dam, the Nile level can be held steady throughout the year, maximising the potential for transport and irrigation although simultaneously creating problems of salination and water supply.

2.1 Geological Origins of Egyptian Landscape

The geological canvas upon which this history of the Nile Valley is placed is one of extreme variation. Full details appear in Said (1981) and are excellently summarised by Sampsell (2014) but, in brief, the rocks of most of Egypt are a stack of more-or-less flat-lying, sedimentary deposits resting upon an ancient crystalline basement. At the base of the sediment layers lie the important aquifers of the Nubian sandstone and above this, layers of chalk and limestone. These were laid down during the geological era of the Cretaceous, around seventy million years ago, in a warm shallow sea. During ice ages when the water level was low in the Mediterranean basin, the Nile cut down through this sandwich of sediments to form a deep canyon with tributary canyons, similar in size to the Grand Canyon. The Egyptian canyon stretched from Aswan in the south to the Mediterranean, or rather the salty and dried-up remains of what was left of it, in the north.

Although the Nile currently has no tributaries in Egypt, in the distant past, when sea level was much lower than today and there was more rain locally, the tributary river valleys were deeply incised into the walls of the canyon through which the Nile flowed (Said 1962,1981 and 1993). Later, when sea levels rose, these valleys became inactive and were choked with sand and gravel from the desert to become the wadis. In the Eastern Desert, these wadis continue to host drought-tolerant plants and fauna as well as the local tribes, creating additional habitable land beyond the Nile Valley (Hobbs 1990). Although rains are rare, perhaps once in ten years, they can cause flash floods when the wadi gravels become fluidised and collapse, carrying gravel, roads and other material with them.

While the wadis form mainly in the flanks of the Nile Valley, to the north in the delta, as sediment was eroded away, mounds of sand were left between the branches of the delta's distributary system. The relict mounds still emerge from the Nile floodplain in the north of Egypt today and are known as the gezirehs, from the Arabic word for island. With rising sea level, the old river valleys refilled and a thin veneer, around 10–20 m thick of rich, black mud was deposited on top of the gravels and around the gezirehs. It is this thin layer of mud upon which the majority of the modern inhabitants of Egypt rely for agriculture and from which they derived the early name for Egypt, *kmt*, the black land. The sandy mounds of the gezirehs became some of the earliest inhabited parts of the delta.

The Nile, as a large river system affected by climate change, responds according to the laws of physics, as any large river does. Borehole investigations reveal that although early humans tracked habitats as the landscape changed, with time they started to understand the river and its behaviour, and intervene, adapting it to their own needs for transport, drinking water, food and irrigation. In exploring this history, we adopt the traditional designations of periods of Egyptian history. For consistency, we have used the ancient chronology used by Shaw (2003) in his *Oxford History of Ancient Egypt* which is summarised as a timeline in Table 1.

2.2 Landscape and Early Egyptology

In a broad sense, it took some time to realise that the landscape provided the missing piece of the archaeological puzzle. Our understanding of Egyptian landscape processes was slow to develop and came from the gradual discovery of the validity of non-written source materials, the development of meaningful methodologies to record these and, finally, a broader knowledge base within the context of historical and geological findings. We note that the earliest excavations in Egypt were preoccupied with the exploration of the then-undeciphered hieroglyphs (Thompson 2015), visible on monuments in Egypt. These

Table 1 The main periods of Egyptian history referred to in this text (with commonly used abbreviations) taken from the timescale of Shaw (2003)

Palaeolithic	*c.* 700,000–5,000 BC
Saharan Neolithic Period	*c.* 8800–4700 BC
Predynastic Period	*c.* 5300–3000 BC
Early Dynastic Period (ED)	*c.* 3000–2686 BC
Old Kingdom (OK)	2686–2160 BC
First Intermediate Period (FIP)	2160–2055 BC
Middle Kingdom (MK)	2055–1650 BC
Second Intermediate Period (SIP)	1650–1550 BC
New Kingdom (NK)	1550–1069 BC
Ramesside Period (subdivision of NK)	1295–1069 BC
Third Intermediate Period (TIP)	1069–664 BC
Late Period	664–332 BC
Ptolemaic Period	332–30 BC
Roman Period	30 BC–395 AD
Byzantine Period	395–619 AD
Persian Empire	619–639 AD
Muslim Dynastic Period	639–1517 AD
Arab and Ottoman Period	639–1882 AD
Khedivate	1882–1953 AD
Republican Period	1953 AD–

monuments, known throughout the world, have long been a subject of scholarship and many ancient visitors recorded their wonder at the achievements of the past in their inscriptions. However, modern Egyptology was initiated in the politics of the late eighteenth century. In 1798, Napoleon, as part of adding Egypt to his Empire, landed a force of 160 scholars alongside the army to collate and propagate knowledge. The 'savants' as they were known, published newspapers and made maps and plans creating a fascinating and detailed catalogue of Egypt at the time. They also discovered the Rosetta Stone which was the key to deciphering hieroglyphs.

The problem for modern geo-archaeologists is that although historically, many objects and artifacts remained intact and preserved, few records of the archaeological and geological context in which they were found were kept. It was not until the late nineteenth century when Hekekyan (1807–75; Jeffreys 2010) and Petrie (1853–1942), among others, began to make detailed observations of the find spots, recording in fascinating detail not only their finds but also what they saw in the surrounding area and what this might tell us. We could perhaps point at this moment in time as the birth of geo-archaeology as a discipline in its own right. Now, modern archaeology takes careful note of the 'context' or sediments in which inscriptions are found, yielding valuable information about the ancient landscape. Perhaps unsurprisingly, given the absence of context for many of the texts, translations of the texts and interpretations of the sites took it for granted that the landscape in which the sites were set had been much as it is now. When Baines and Malek (1980) compiled their atlas of ancient Egypt, they realised that, as there was so little information about how the Nile moved, they were obliged to portray it in its modern course, regardless of the period and the ancient geography.

Caton-Thompson (1932 and 1952) in the early twentieth century suggested that the environment had not always been what it is today. The geologist in her team, Gardner, observed from sediments associated with the ruins that they had been built in wetter times. Soon afterwards, during the 1960s, there was a major campaign of rescue archaeology preceding the inundation of a large part of Nubia with the waters of the reservoir, Lake Nasser. From these surveys, further prehistoric discoveries were made including those by Wendorf and Schild (1998) at Nabta Playa in the Nubian Desert some 800 km south of Cairo. From their excavations, Wendorf and Schild could see how strategic lakeshore sites were reoccupied multiple times, even though the traces of earlier occupation were shallowly buried and no longer visible. The fact that ancient sand dunes, buried in the lake mud, had contained reservoirs of fresh water provided further evidence of the importance of these fresh-water sources to prehistoric humans. In fact, the presence of these lakes was a crucial consideration in the occupational patterns of prehistoric humans and those that followed them, as we will show later.

The exploration in the 1980s and 1990s of the large and significant sites of Tell El-Dab'a and Piramesse by Manfred Bietak, who incidentally also participated in the Aswan Dam rescue excavations, highlighted a series of waterways that had connected these sites (Bietak 2017). Around the same time, Butzer, working in the Nile Valley at the Pyramids of Giza started to apply the evidence from sediments around historic sites to understanding their environment. A mathematician, geographer, meteorologist and archaeologist, his seminal work on the Nile Valley in 1976, *Early Hydraulic Civilization in Egypt: A Study in Cultural Ecology*, set the scene for modern investigations where sediment logs and boreholes are now considered a routine part of archaeological investigation.

This type of investigation was taken up by others (Jeffreys 1985; Stanley and Warne 1993 and 1994) who augmented the parallel explorations of Attia (1954) and his teams on behalf of the Geological Survey of Egypt. Similarly, Stanley and Warne (1994) used carbon dates and more than a hundred boreholes (the extraction of columns of soil samples to examine subsurface deposits in order to complete a picture of site use over time) to explore the development and architecture of marine deltas from different parts of the world. Around the same time, Jeffreys added a programme of auger coring to the work of the Survey of Memphis (Jeffreys 1985), in order to contextualise previous excavations into the broader landscape. Over the ensuing thirty years, his team cored and logged at hundreds of locations totalling more than two kilometres of sediment. As they went, they trained a battalion of students in the art of logging and landscape interpretation who have since worked at many sites across Egypt.

2.3 Landscape in Egypt

Broadly, Egypt can be divided into four main types of environment: the Delta to the North, the Nile Valley running through the centre, and the deserts and oases that flank it. Within these environments, landscape change is relatively slow; for example, the Nile migration that is perceptible over a few generations (Bunbury et al. 2008 ; Lutley and Bunbury 2008) or the desertification of the Sahara that lasted around a millennium (Kröpelin et al. 2008 ; Kupar and Kröpelin 2006). On an even longer timescale, the Delta, swamped by rising sea levels, reached its marshiest around 6000 BC and spent the following 3,000–4,000 years reconsolidating its channels to form the topography we see today (Pennington et al. 2016). Figure 2 shows the changes to the main habitats: the Delta, the Nile Valley, the Oases and the deserts. Black diamonds identify points at which

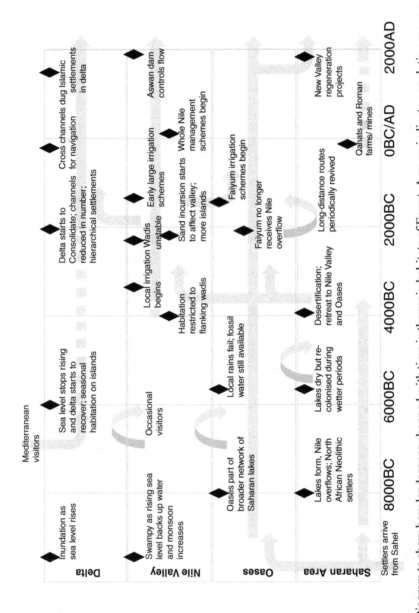

Figure 2 Diagram to show how landscapes changed with time in the main habitats of Egypt. Arrows indicate population movements between habitats and diamonds indicate events in the landscape evolution documented in the archaeological record.

changes are recorded in the archaeological record and the grey arrows show how human patterns of habitation and migration have responded to the changing environment. The Nile Valley has been a habitat into and out of which ancient Egyptians migrated and which we will explore in more detail here. For those living in Egypt, these habitats are intimately connected and their constant attachment to these areas demonstrates the significance of these sites in providing the basics for life and the building blocks for a new civilisation.

Even though much of landscape change is slow, gradual change to a habitat may mean that it reaches a tipping point. For example, for those people living around the Saharan playas in the late predynastic (around 4000–3600 BC), the deterioration of the food source when the sites dried up, forced many people into the Nile Valley. This condensation of population also, as we will see, had a dramatic impact on those already resident there. Further north in the Delta in another example, a change from very rich and diverse habitats towards a more monotonous set of channels was a driver for a more hierarchical society managed from Memphis, the node at which they met. Or, similarly, in the Nile Valley, a period of unpredictable weather in the New Kingdom, with high Nile and flash floods in the nearby desert, inspired the development of a landscape-wide system of channels and reservoirs in Luxor.

3 The Early Holocene Climate Seesaw

The Nile Valley and Delta were rather inhospitable during the wet phases of the early Holocene since river levels were high and the annual summer flood brought by the Ethiopian monsoon was also larger. Furthermore, local rainfall in Egypt contributed to the generally wet conditions. Towards the end of the Saharan Neolithic, both flood levels and local rainfall were reduced rendering the Nile tamer while at the same time, the reduction in local rainfall in the Saharan region drove people out of the deserts making the Nile a popular destination. Flanking the Nile, the wadis were well vegetated and provided ready access to the desert as did the terraces that flanked the marshes of the Delta. A combination of hunting in the wadis, with fishing and gathering in the Nile Valley, was augmented by some herding of sheep, goats and cattle. When seasonal rains refreshed the Sahara, the wadis also provided easy access to the lakes and playas (seasonal lakes). The Nile, now the life-blood of Egypt, began its rise to supreme importance.

The Nile and its expanse of catchment have been globally significant to the civilisations and cultures of the region for millennia, providing an important corridor for the movement of people and animals throughout the Holocene. Flowing for over 6,000 km from the south of the Equator to the shores of the

Mediterranean and covering an area of 3 million square kilometres, it is unique both in size and variety of river basin. The main contributors to the Nile in Egypt are the White Nile that rises in equatorial Africa and the Blue Nile that rises in the Highlands of Ethiopia: these join at Khartoum in Sudan. The Nile is unusual that it has few other perennial tributaries meaning that its character is remarkably similar for much of its course northwards from Khartoum. The catchment supports a vast range of ecosystems and has played a central role in the development of a rich diversity of communities.

The Nile floodplain in Egypt currently forms a green cultivated strip that cuts north–south across the Sahara Desert. To many, the river appears immutable but the current form is the result of a tempestuous past. The river today is the result of many phases of development (Said 1981) but for our purposes it is sufficient to begin six million years ago with the erosion of what is described as the Nile Canyon, the valley bounded by cliffs through which the Nile flows. The meandering of the modern Nile is constrained by this canyon to a narrow strip no more than 12 km wide.

During the annual flood cycle, the White Nile maintains a steady flow but the Blue Nile, with its highly seasonal swelling of waters from the Ethiopian monsoon, causes an annual inundation (for more details, see Woodward et al. 2007). Small wonder that life in the Nile Valley started to revolve around the flood and the seasons were determined by it. First came Akhet (June to September) when the floodwaters rose and no farming could take place although mass-transport of goods could occur since the water was deeper and more extensive than at other times of the year. As the flood receded, it ushered in the season of Peret (October to February) when as much of the land as possible was used for agriculture. Activities included sowing and reaping crops in the irrigated flood-basins as well as grazing of stock or even hunting in the thickets and marshes that fringed the valley. By March, the harvest was ready and Shemu (March to May) began. Once the crops were in, preparation for the next flood season began; clearing ditches and repairing embankments ready for the flood to return.

Although we can no longer observe the annual flood of the Nile, fortunately, we still have historic maps and travellers' accounts as well as the exceptional photographic record of Lehnert and Landrock who ran a photographic business in Cairo during the early twentieth century and who photographed the Nile from all angles and in all seasons. For example, in their image of Dashur, the settlement huddled on a piece of high ground, appears to be a ship afloat in the floodwaters of the Nile Valley while a photograph of the Pyramids at Giza taken at a similar time of year shows boats approaching the monuments. Although the inundation became a regular feature of life on the Nile, climatic change meant that there were times of high and low flood. Macklin and his co-workers (Macklin et al. 2015) suggest that these recent effects of climate change on the Nile can be divided into five significant stages (Table 2), characterised by major changes and shifts in lake levels and river flows. Even though the seasonality of the Nile floods did not change during the Holocene, the magnitude of flood events changed considerably and progressively as climate changed (Macklin et al. 2015). Sudden reductions in river flow caused widespread channel and floodplain contraction and these events recurred frequently over the course of 6,000–7,000 years affecting riverine societies dramatically.

During periods of low global temperature, the Ethiopian monsoon is reduced and, during the last ice glacial maximum, even switched off so that the Nile is fed only by the White Nile. Conversely, with global temperatures higher, as they are now, the Ethiopian monsoon, with its consequent inundation, is restored. Local rainfall that falls in Egypt, during times of higher global temperature, augments the Nile rushing into it from the wadis (Rodrigues et al. 2000; Stanley et al. 2003). In Ethiopia, the monsoon erodes the basalts of the Highlands adding dark-red mud to the Nile which turns the river red as it travels down to Egypt, arriving between June and October. As the river channel becomes very full it eventually spills over the river's natural levees and spreads across the flood-plain. At times of very intense inundation, Nile water broadens into the mouths of neighbouring wadis, extending the cultivable area of the Nile floodplain.

The changing impact of the river on the cultures and beliefs of the peoples of the region can be seen throughout the last 5,000 years, in literature and in art. These span the years from the ancient Egyptians and great-irrigation-based civilisations, with their strong association and dependence on the river, to the modern-day Egyptians who strive to manage, harvest and control the Nile's vast power through dam construction (Woodward et al. 2007). Stanley and Warne (1994) posit that it was the maturation of deltas near sea level that gave rise to civilisations across the globe as sea levels stabilised in the mid-Holocene after a period of rapid rise (Pennington 2016). Together with these successful and long-living civilisations came developments in agricultural practices and the emergence of more complex social organisations, arguably as a response to the climatic changes that they were experiencing at the time. Studies of areas close to the Nile, such as Faiyum, demonstrate similar patterns with periods of occupation and abandonment throughout the Holocene.

3.1 Human Adaption in Response to the Change in Climate

Farming and herding in the Nile Valley began around the late sixth millennium BC. Macklin et al. (2015) explores the correlation of adoption of

Table 2 Stages in the development of the Nile

Stage	Date	Nile behaviour	Human movements (see also Table 1)
1	6,400 – 5,800 cal. BC	Significant hydrological variability, characterised by high to low water levels in key lakes contracting channels and floodplain due to drier conditions and reduced flow.	Episodic occupation of desert lakes and playas with seasonal visits to Nile Valley.
2	4,500 cal. BC	Next major shift in Nile catchment, falling temperatures in Kilimanjaro and low water levels in Lake Victoria and Tana, and coinciding with diminishing river flows in the Nile delta.	Increasing shift of habitation towards Nile Valley and wadi mouths and terraces that connect with it. Early stages of state formation and irrigation management begin.
3	2,800 – 2,450 cal. BC	Falling water levels and decreasing flow and cooler temperatures.	Saharan habitation restricted to wadi ranges. Concentration of population into Nile Valley and onto river levees of the Nile. Nile and minor channel management begins.
4	After 450 cal. BC	Water levels never exceed those recorded before 500 cal. BC.	Occasional recrudescences of Saharan trade activity. Whole Nile management schemes intensify.
5	1450–1650 cal. AD	Falling and low lake levels in the Blue Nile and decreasing flows in the Nile Delta.	Human activity focussed on Nile Valley; only sparse trans-desert trade routes persist.

new farming practises and the development and success of new civilisations with changes in climate, in particular channel and floodplain contraction. Macklin speculates that a period of river-channel contraction would be advantageous to farmers by exposing nutrient-rich sediment on the floodplain and making the exposed areas less hazardous and more manageable for agriculture. An analogous way of life persists among the Bedouin of the Eastern Desert of Egypt today. Joseph Hobbs (1990) describes a way of life in which the Bedouin use local knowledge to navigate the desert, anticipating where rain had fallen and where water could be found at different times of the year. Through a mixture of harvesting resources and pasturing their flocks where fodder could be found, the Bedouin are able to subsist in the wilderness (Murray 1935). At times, anticipating future rains, they plant seeds in a basin and, without tilling the crop, they hope to return at a later time to find a harvest, a sort of minimalist agriculture.

The development of farming and riverine societies in the Nile Valley in the late sixth millennium BC was far later than in SW Asia (Kuper and Kropelin 2006). The transition to the Neolithic economy occurred after a major period of channel and floodplain contraction between 6150 and 5750 cal. BC, coinciding with drier conditions. This was advantageous as nutrients and rich sediments were spread across former floodplains. The channels consequently became less hazardous, more exposed and more manageable for farmers. In Kerma (Welsby 2001) in Upper Nubia, after 5300 BC there was a shift of occupation to alluvial plains which had been previously unoccupied. This shift was associated with the aridification of the local environment although Nile records indicate Neolithic settlements of the valley floor coincided with higher river flows than prior to 7,500 cal. BC.

Unfortunately, within the Nile Valley and delta, evidence for early farming in the diverse habitats of the maturing river system are scarce or non-existent due to the rapid sedimentation in this area that buries the evidence (Pennington et al. 2016; Yann Tristant 2004 and unpublished book) before 2000 BC. However, areas where there is large movement of mineral material are those that have the most fertile soils. For example, Vesuvius, an active volcano on the Italian peninsula, that although cataclysmically dangerous, provides very fertile soils which have supported vibrant human populations, or similarly, the actively faulting basins of Western Turkey that present the perfect growing environment for fruit and other foodstuffs. We expect that the diverse habitats of the Nile Valley were ideal for fishing and fowling supported by harvesting of wild grains.

As the immature river system gave way to a more mature river system with lower environmental diversity and more stable channels, this habitat became less fertile and required the adoption of agricultural practices and techniques in the delta that also spread to the floodplains (Pennington et al. 2016). Hence, changing diets were a notable feature of this transition: earlier reliance was on aquatic resources and fish, in particular, were enormously important with remains of burnt fish prevalent, for example, at Sais in the Nile Delta (Wilson 2006). There are also prolific offerings of fish at temples during this time in contrast to a relative absence of mammals or any complex or highly developed animal husbandry techniques. After the stabilisation of the channels this appears to no longer be the case (Pennington et al. 2016).

Some scholars, for example Kupar and Kröpelin (2006), identify the see-sawing of climate between warm, humid conditions and cooler, arid conditions as the motor of evolution in North Africa. As people begin to control the cycle of grasses and other plants, they select and sow varieties that meet their requirements. Thus, the involvement of farmers causes adaptation of wild grasses, for example wheat, that have a higher yield even if this means that they are more intensive to farm. Ethnobotanists who study botanical remains from archaeological sites, including the burnt grains in remains from hearths, see a change in the plants as domestication proceeds. For Egypt, its neighbours, in this case to the north-east in Mesopotamia, had already developed domesticated species which could conveniently be imported to the Egyptian Delta. Phillips (Phillips et al. 2012) suggests that people adopted the domestic grains when environmentally viable and sensible to do so, meaning that the changing environmental conditions triggered drastic changes in agricultural adoption.

As the deserts dried, Saharan communities continued to flourish but were concentrated into the residual wet areas. These were terraces of sediment fringing the river floodplain, the flanking wadis and the oases. The remaining grasslands of the hinterland still provided ample food when combined with a diet rich in fish, sourced from the Nile. By the Early Dynastic Period, unification swept across Egypt, forging both north and south into one political entity under the leadership of Hierakonpolis, a large site on the Saharan bank of the Nile near Edfu. This innovation may reflect the concentration of people and resources into the Nile Valley from the encroaching desert (Kuper and Kropelin 2006), perhaps providing evidence of the impact of environmental change on populations and the link between changes in societal structure and events within the broader landscape. At this time, the wadis were still eminently habitable (see Figure 3) and, thanks to the protective vegetation that reduced the impact of rainfall, there was little run off or sand erosion.

Hierakonpolis is an example, par excellence, of a site at the transition from life adjacent to the Nile to life in the Nile Valley (Bunbury and Graham 2008; Dufton and Branton 2009). There is evidence for continuous habitation there

Figure 3 Vegetation in modern Peruvian Wadis showing how we imagine the wadis around Hierakonpolis during the heyday of the site. Photo Nicholas Warner.

from the predynastic to the New Kingdom but it is for the predynastic excep-tional finds that Nekhen (later known as Hierakonpolis) is best known. The site is dominated by a very large mud-brick enclosure, known as the Khasekhemwy Enclosure. Early excavations by Quibell and Green (Quibell 1900) in the late nineteenth century revealed many rare items including ripple-flaked, flint knives that had been turned pink by heat treatment. They were too large to have been of more than ceremonial use and were accompanied by a ceremonial mace-head and schist palette attributed to Narmer, one of the early Kings of Egypt. The early excavations have been followed by many other investigations (Adams 1995; Hoffman et al. 1986) that have revealed wooden buildings, elephant and baboon burials and many other discoveries. As the elephants seem to have died quite young, they are suspected to be imported animals. Abundant rhizocretions at the site indicate that the silt terraces that flank the Nile were well vegetated in the past, sustained by local rainfall during the mid-Holocene (Hoffman et al. 1986) and therefore relatively stable.

Exploration by augering at the site of Hierakonpolis around the temple and the wadi mouth revealed some fascinating insights into the fluctuating land-scape in the area. In the late predynastic, the island flank became subject to incursions of desert clay during wadi-wash events. So, by the predynastic the wadis were perceived as the ideal site for habitation but this did not last. At the same time as the Nile channels were stabilising, the opposite was true for the wadis that flanked the Nile. When rainfall is plentiful, vegetation stabilises the wadi floor and absorbs water, preventing erosion of the sediments. As rainfall drops and vegetation becomes sparse, the wadis flow, causing destabilisation of the wadi sands and gravel. Increased habitation led to further demands on the land around the wadis, which inadvertently reduced vegetation in the area. The evidence for wooden architecture (www.hierakonpolis-online.org/) at Hierakonpolis suggests that the denudation was assisted by humans who felled trees, culled firewood for brewing and baking (Adams 1995) and grazed animals over shrubs and grasses leading to wadi wash-out and destabilisation. At Hierakonpolis, boreholes show evidence for three successive collapses, each more dramatic than the previous one. As conditions become more arid, the rate of erosion drops (Goudie and Wilkinson 1977). Eventually, although all the vegetation is dead, there is no longer any rainfall to erode the sediment and the wadi becomes relatively stable again.

A similar pattern of erosion is seen elsewhere in Egypt. Work by El-Sanussi and Jones (1997) in the area of west Cairo show a pattern of wadi-washouts that produced tongues of sandy sediment that intruded the muds of the Nile Valley (Figure 4). They reveal that the early settlements from the Maadi period (*c.*3900–3300 BC) were in the wadis that flanked the Nile Valley. Some of these settlements were washed away while others were buried by the sediment flowing down. Later on, during the Old Kingdom at Giza (Lehner et al. 2009), the wadi through Khentkawes town was again eroded as water rushed down the wadi and later repaired. With time, settlements in the flanking wadis were destroyed or abandoned as the ground became unstable, forcing inhabitants to move instead to the banks of the Nile. Elsewhere, remains of Badarian and other Early Dynastic settlements survive in the wadi mouths where the desert catchments disgorge into the Nile Valley (Dufton and Branton 2009). What is clear is that occupants of the area even then, some 1,000 years prior to the supposed dramatic climate chaos of the First Intermediate Period, were adapting to changing landscape and climate.

With life in the Nile Valley stabilising and the deserts increasingly hostile, forays to the known sources of raw materials, particularly precious stone, became hazardous and labour intensive. It required a powerful king like Khafra, pharaoh in the Fourth Dynasty of the Old Kingdom (*c.*2750 BC), to send missions into the desert for example to Gebel el-Asr, an area known for the 'Cephren diorite quarries', far away in the south of Egypt (Shaw et al. 2001). The area, close to the border with Sudan was around 800 km from the great Pyramid of Khafra at Giza where he used the stone won from the quarries (Figure 5). The Old Kingdom quarries at the site indicate the extent to which the climate and landscape have changed.

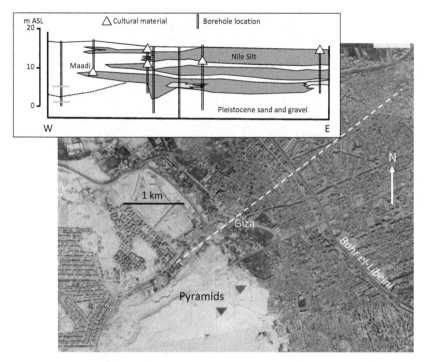

Figure 4 Map taken from GoogleEarth shows location of section and east–west section after Branton (2008) and Senussi and Jones (1997) of wadi sediments is inset. Note how three successive tongues of sediment (white) invade the sediments of the Nile Valley (grey).

Excavations also show that in the Old Kingdom, the site was supported by wells, and brewing and baking were conducted in an area near Quartz Ridge. The surface into which the sledge tracks and wells were cut also hosted aestivating snails, *zootechus insularis*, a species that can endure seven years of drought and is known for surviving in museums for years before a period of humidity stimulates them to move around inside the display cases (e.g. at the British Museum). These small snails are another indicator of the relatively mild climate of the site at the time of Khafra since, by this time, the Sahel had not retreated as far south as it later did (Kröplin et al. 2008). The most likely route for the egress of the sledges from the site is through the Wadi Toshka, the same spillway that formerly fed the Khargan Basin and into the Nile Valley in Nubia, an area now flooded by Lake Nasser.

The quarries were reused during the Middle Kingdom but workshops and storerooms were by then tightly clustered around a settlement at Quartz Ridge with a large number of storage jars being used by the expedition. Even though amongst these jars – later sealed by sand – a bird's nest indicated milder

Figure 5 Trackways of a loading ramp for the 'Cephren diorite Quarry' at Gebel al-Asr cut into lake muds and constructed from striped blocks of the same diorite that was used for the statues at Khafra's pyramid at Giza.

conditions than today, the impression is more of a fully provisioned mission than a seasonal settlement. The Middle Kingdom route to the Nile, rather than take the long way around through the Wadi Toshka, was a donkey trail marked by cairns that made its way to the closest point in the Nile Valley (Bloxham 1998). The material extracted at this period was exclusively for smaller pieces such as bowls and jars and many of the latter are found in Egypt associated with the rite of the 'opening of the mouth', part of the funerary ritual. At Gebel al-Asr, laminated wind-blown sand, characteristic of the early phase of sand release from the Sahara, encapsulates the Middle Kingdom remains even though, in the north at Giza, in the time of Khafra, it had already started to enclose buildings of the earlier periods.

In summary, during the final stages of aridification of the Sahara, the wadis that impinged upon the Nile eroded at a faster rate, adding sand and gravel to the Nile Valley, raising the floodplain. The new sediment also infilled marshes and channels and gradually reduced them to a few main arteries. Although the channels still moved, they did so more by migration (meandering) than by jumping (avulsion) as the multiple channels that preceded them had done. These new stable channels built larger levees rising two metres or more above the surrounding floodplain to become attractive spots for settlement. They were close to the river but safe from the flood. By the same token, in the delta, the previously isolated sand islands (gezireh) also became more accessible as the channels and marshes between them began to fill. Early inhabitants, ever fearful of the destructive nature of the Nile, sought out land on high promontories that could afford them refuge from the seasonal floods; the shores of these islands provided the necessary protection for both the living and the dead. Early populations, who had previously made the desert their home and only occasionally visited the Nile, now moved to the cusp of the desert and the river habitats. They made the Nile Valley and the Delta their permanent home, beginning the process of turning their back forever on their desert existence.

4 The Old Kingdom

The location of the King's court known as 'the residence' changed frequently in Ancient Egypt. Although these settlements were more regal estates than cities in the modern sense (Ragazzoli 2011), I will call them 'cities' here for brevity. The move into the Nile Valley in the Old Kingdom sparked the formation of the earliest cities around Giza (Lehner 2009). The focus moved from the Old and Middle Kingdom to Memphis, also in the north, then southwards to Thebes during the New Kingdom. From Thebes, there was an excursion to Amarna before the return to Memphis, demonstrating the complex interplay of politics, geology, climate and demography over time. As the Saharan area declined in importance, populations settled down to a cosy existence in the Nile Valley. During the Old Kingdom, settlements and estate-towns were restricted to the safe high ground of the levees and islands. These levees were long, low swells fringing the Nile and its former channels so the settlements were strung out along them and confined to the tops during the flood (Jeffreys and Tavares 1994). As the floodwaters receded, agricultural and pastoral activity spread out into the surrounding floodplain. Occasional wetter periods reanimated interest in the deserts, until Roman and Islamic times (Shaw et al. 1999; Shaw et al. 2001), in particular from mining expeditions, but there was generally insufficient water for permanent residence. The wadi mouths and the nearby desert still supported sufficient drought-tolerant game to act as a hunting range so despite permanent migration to the levees and the floodplains, there were still occasional sorties into the desert for food and mineral extraction.

Eventually, towards the end of the Old Kingdom, the vegetation died and wind-blown sand from the Sahara started to drift into the Nile Valley in the north, masking the topography, infilling channels and creating dune-fields over some of the Nile silts (Alexanian et al. 2011; Verstraeten et al. 2017). The blown sand gradually mantled areas further and further to the south until by the end of the Middle Kingdom the whole of Egypt was blanketed with sand (Shaw et al. 2001). The sand incursion led to further floodplain rise and greater consolidation of the delta. The effects of the consolidation of the delta will be explored in more detail in the following.

Overall, the long-range trend from the mid-Holocene was one of gradual desiccation as drying commenced in the north and continued southwards (Kuper and Kröpelin 2006). However, local microclimates and short-range temperature excursions from the trend meant that the associated landscape changes were not synchronised across Egypt. Evidence discussed here shows the kinds of landscape changes that affected the Nile Valley as a result of climate cycling. We have divided Egypt into four main habitats: In the north, the Delta, and to the south, the Nile Valley. The valley is surrounded by the Saharan area itself punctuated by a fourth habitat, the oases. There is a complex interplay between the four areas but for simplicity, we have described the history of each area in turn. Figure 2 summarises some of the main events in the landscape history and maps the movement of people from habitats that have become inhospitable to those that have become more attractive.

5 The First Intermediate Period

The culmination of the drying of the Saharan region came during the First Intermediate Period (FIP) which is often looked upon as a dark time – a time of adjustment, chaos and political disorder in stark contrast to the wealth and harmony that existed during the Old Kingdom. Middle Kingdom literature initiated this view by recalling apocalyptical events, failing floods and incipient riots, as do some more recent authors (Hassan, 1996). The FIP also coincided with low floods, seen in evidence from the Qarun Lake levels of the Faiyum Depression; continued encroachment of sand brought forth by winds in the Sahara; tropical trees displaced by Sahel-type trees and decay of sporadic vegetation; and rainfall below 150 mm/yr (Kropelin et al. 2008). Coupled with observations of sands (Goncalves 2019) and flood deposits around Memphis towards the end of the Old Kingdom, we may posit that the addition of abundant sediment to the Nile generated an increased number of islands in the river and produced a period of enhanced floodplain rise. The additional sediment also hastened the maturation of the delta accompanied by movement of the delta-head northwards, as supported by the work of Pryer (2011; Bunbury et al. 2017).

However, the literature presents a view of the chaos that was formed in the Memphis area and archaeological work further south at Edfu (Moeller 2005) and at Dendara (Wendrich, personal communication) suggest that southern Egypt was not affected by famine or sand influx at the end of the Old Kingdom.

It is unsurprising then that the ancient Egyptians, now becoming so inevitably bound to the Nile, became interested in measuring and recording flood heights and taking measures, both secular and spiritual, to control the river (Bell 1970). Their preoccupation with Nile behaviour can be seen from the earliest writings from the predynastic onwards. From the beginning of the Old Kingdom (2700 BC), efforts were directed towards recording and predicting Nile levels year-on-year. Observations of the peak height of the flood were essential to the management of irrigation systems and to the setting of the tax levels for the forthcoming harvests. The extensive tax records of the Wilbour Papyrus from the New Kingdom demonstrate how complex land registration and tax-ation systems had become by that period (Antoine 2017). Other literature, also from the same period, provides ample evidence of the changes in Nile levels at the time and the lengths to which ancient Egyptians went to monitor and control its flow.

Beyond these records of the annual cycle, an early Middle Kingdom text, the 'Prophecy of Neferti' (Lichtheim 1973) suggests that there was already a perception of longer-range environmental change, while by the time of Herodotus (440 BC; see Dewald 1998) there were reports of lake levels in the Faiyum being different from those in the time of King Moeris, 900 years earlier. In fact, one could argue that the Egyptian 'media' were as preoccupied with Nile behaviour as Britons are with the weather. Years of abundant floods are con-firmed in the story 'Instructions of Amenemhat', a poem detailing a conversation between a dead pharaoh and his son, written in the time of the Middle Kingdom. It tells of excess of food and the success of harvests:

It was I who brought forth grain, the grain god loved me,
the Nile adored me from his every source;
One did not hunger during my years, did not thirst;
they sat content with all my deeds, remembering me fondly;
and I set each thing firmly in its place. [Translated Parkinson 1991]

In addition to the textual evidence, other evidence from animal remains in owl pellets shows that, during the Old Kingdom, those deposited in the tombs of Saqqara were those of owls that had dined on damp-loving species of mice and frogs/toads. By the Middle Kingdom, owl diets had changed to one of aridity-tolerant species, such as gerbils and desert toads (Pokorny et al. 2009). In addition to the fauna, the flora of the desert also suffered and was dried out. Now that the roots no longer protected the sandy wadi-beds from erosion and the leaves no longer sheltered the sand from the erosive power of a cloudburst, water and sand rushing down the valley could sweep away large quantities of sediment as long as there were still rainstorms. With time, even the rainstorms failed and, although erosion slowed down, restricted to wind erosion or deflation, people turned their backs on the desert. It is interesting to speculate whether the increasingly poor reputation of the desert-god Seth, once an equal if opposite partner of Horus, was related to increasingly negative attitudes to the now denuded deserts. Figure 6 shows a late image of the king destroying Seth, by now a diminutive hippopotamus, from the Ptolemaic temple of Edfu.

At the same time that the Nile was becoming tamer, the increasing dryness of the Saharan region was releasing fossil sand dunes that had been stabilised by plants into the wind. This sand, carried by the trade winds, flowed into the Nile

Figure 6 King destroying Seth from the Ptolemaic temple of Edfu.

Valley where it was deposited into the river before being carried downstream to form islands in the Nile and also to hasten the consolidation of the delta after its early Holocene inundation.

6 The Delta

Although today approximately one third of Egypt's population lives in the Delta, 8,000 years ago during the Saharan Neolithic Period, the delta was much smaller and had been inundated by the sea as ice caps melted at the end of the ice age. The aridification of the Saharan region and the influx of sand to the Nile Valley had a downstream effect on the delta creating the landscape we see today. The extra sand stabilised river channels, a process that gradually propagated through the delta moving coast-wards. The rapid influx of sand between the Old and New Kingdoms accelerated this process but created a habitat poorer in nutrients. The need to glean food from a wider area was an additional factor in spurring urbanisation (Pennington et al. 2016).

Global sea levels rose at the end of the last ice age 12,500 years ago (Fairbanks 1989) meaning that sea-level deltas across the world have evolved in roughly parallel ways (Stanley and Warne 1994; Figure 7). The additional water from the melted ice sheets initially pushed the coastline of the deltas inland. Upstream of the old coast, fresh water from the river system was held

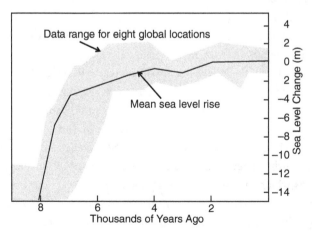

Figure 7 Global average sea-level curve showing how there was a steep rise in sea level after the end of the last ice age that slowed around 6–7000 years ago. After Flemming et al. 1999 and Robert Rohde's (2006) climate change art compilation. As a result of the interplay between subsidence and sea-level change in the Nile Delta, it is not considered a representative locality and is therefore not included.

back forming marshes and swamps far inland. The number of distributary branches in this marshy landscape also increased since channels divide to form distributaries when the base of the main channel reaches sea level. Sea level continued to rise until around 6,000 years ago when the deltas started to recover. With time and sediment supply from the hinterland, the marshes were once again reduced to small pockets and the coastline moved offshore again. The rate of sediment supply and the geometry of the sea floor close to the river mouth are the key factors influencing this process (Pennington 2016). Thus, although not exactly in synchrony, the world's sea-level deltas all recovered from inundation by the sea through a series of similar environments. Reports from the informants of Herodotus (*c.*440 BCE) even tell us that 'the Nile overflowed all Egypt below Memphis'.

Since other deltas are subject to the same processes, we can compare the evolution of the Nile Valley with models derived from more intensively studied deltas such as the Rhine (Berendsen and Stouthamer 2001; Makaske 1998) and the Mississippi (Aslan and Autin 1999). There is a wealth of geographical data for the Rhine with data collected from 180,000 or more boreholes (Toonen 2013) sunk in the area by generations of geography students. This excellent dataset can be used to understand the new Holocene delta of the Nile that overlaid an earlier Pleistocene delta produced by previous oscillations of sea level during the Pleistocene.

Interpolating data already acquired for the Nile Delta with the theoretical models, Ben Pennington (Pennington et al. 2016) shows that we should expect a very rich habitat for humans in the early dynastic (approx. 3100 BC to 2600 BC) but that, with time, as the delta began to grow again, the level of nutrients available in the environment will decrease. Between 4000–2000 BC, spanning the predynastic and Old Kingdom, the original marshy environments became marginalised to the coastal region of the delta as channels became fewer and better-defined turning into meandering channels. These environments are known as the large-scale crevassing stage (LSC) and the meandering stage (Figure 8). During large scale crevassing (A), rivers are flanked by natural sandy levees which may be breached by the river to create crevasse deposits. There are many islands and pockets of low ground in which water collects forming marshy areas within the floodplain. The islands and bars of the river are constantly shifting as material is eroded and then deposited. During meandering (B), the river is contained within a single migrating channel. Bars form on the inside of bends which migrate outwards and downstream in a similar manner to the Nile in Upper Egypt discussed previously. As meandering develops, crevasse deposits become rare and the floodplain is better drained with fewer marshy pockets.

Large-scale crevassing

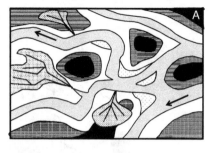

KEY

- River
- Sand bars
- Crevasse (flood) deposits
- Floodbasins
- River levées
- Floodplain deposits

Meandering

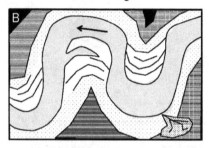

Figure 8 Diagram (after Pennington et al. 2016; Weerts 1996) to show the environments encountered during (A), the large-scale crevassing stage of delta development and (B), the meandering stage.

As a result of this process, the number of distributary channels began to decrease and the network of channels became less well connected (Stanley and Warne 1993). This meant that the delta changed towards the modern geometry with distributaries reducing in number and radiating from a single point in the general area of Cairo, often known as the 'delta head' in Egypt. Figure 9 shows how the initially rich network of habitats and channels of the LSC supported a large number of small communities each of which could travel more-or-less directly from any one to any other. As meandering replaced the LSC, gradually propagating north, food resources became sparse in the interior of the delta and the interconnectivity of the channel network was reduced. At this time, settlements required resources from a larger area to survive and, by the Old Kingdom, we see a hierarchy of settlements developing with the capital at Memphis in a commanding position at the head of the delta.

Unfortunately, we know little of the early history of the delta since much of it is buried; the predynastic occupation of the delta cannot be definitively determined (Tristant 2004). Examples that we do have, such as the predynastic part of the town of Buto, have been encountered at depth as the final stage of

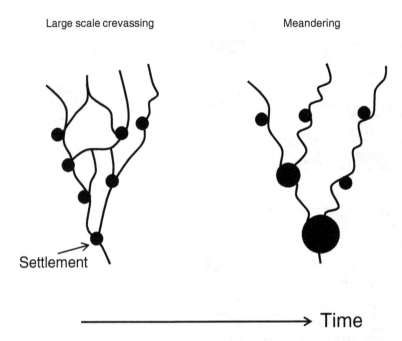

Figure 9 Diagram (after Pennington et al. 2016) to show how the LSC, predominant before 2000 BC, fostered abundant, well-fed and well-connected settlements while the transition to meandering channels, after 2000 BC, favoured the development of larger settlements at the nodes of the Delta distributary system.

excavation of later sites that rise above the delta sediments. Known predynastic sites are often below the current water table in areas where the later accumulations of settlement have been removed; for example, at Sais where Penny Wilson used de-watering equipment to reach the remains of predynastic settlements beneath the site of Sais at Sa El-Hagar (Wilson 2006) and at Kom el-Khilgan (Buchet and Midant-Reynes 2007). Other sites such as Naukratis cannot be further excavated to determine whether there is a core of earlier settlement due to the high groundwater levels. Buto's privileged location at the edge of a morass meant that it retained a supply of fresh water and avoided the *barari*, barren lands that are subject to salt-water conditions in winter and fresh-water conditions in summer.

The better-known contemporaries of these turtle-back sites are those that flanked the delta on higher ground; for example, Merimde Beni Salama where evidence for high bio-diversity in the adjacent swampy habitat is provided by the hippo-tibia steps (steps made out of hippo leg bones) of houses in the settlement (Eiwanger 1992). Micro-predators in the form of parasites and other pathogens were no doubt also abundant in the marshy areas (Groube 1996) – living in this area was a case of eat and be eaten.

Sedimentation through the mouths of the Nile generated delta lobes of their own, such as the one where the Damietta branch debouches into the sea. Long-shore drift where the prevailing currents sweep sediment eastwards around the Mediterranean created sandbars along the coastline. The bars blocked the mouths of the embayments between the mouths of the Nile and created lagoons of which Lake Maryut, Lake Idku, Lake Borollos and Lake Manzala persist today (Stanley and Warne 1994). The lakes provided an important access to port cities like Tinnis during the rougher weather of the sailing season (Cooper 2014) which coincided with the period of the flood that rendered the lagoons fresh. Access to the lagoons was through cuts in the beach bar that in many cases were fortified (e.g. the gate of Tinnis).

The works of Stanley and Warne (1994) and Krom and Stanley (2003) provide our best insight into the subsurface structure of the delta. The latter investigation included some 140 boreholes around the margin of the delta in which they could see evidence for the former mouths of the Nile channel and the effects of marine incursion into the coastal areas. Drill coring at Merimde Beni Salama (Rowland et al. 2014) showed that there is red-mud typical of a body of Nile-supplied still water at around 4 m below the modern delta surface. The Neolithic activity at the site is located on the promontory created by the Wadi Gamal adjacent to this lake and we conclude that this site was at the margins of a large swamp, probably the home of the hippopotami who provided the bones for the door steps and backed by a slightly greener 'desert' than today.

The locations of predynastic sites are likely to have been dictated by the availability of fresh water throughout the year. At some coastal settlements like Alexandria, fossil water stored in the ancient beach ridges provided some degree of water security, while at Merimde Beni Salama, local pools were likely to have been fresh water and replenished by rains flowing down the Wadi Gamal. In the interior of the delta, the high Nile of the flood season ensured a summer fresh water supply but, during the winter the lowered Nile allowed salt-water incursion. By Roman and Mediaeval times, the site of Tinnis was storing fresh water available in the summer in cisterns (Gascoigne 2007) for use during the winter. In the more extreme case of Al-Farama (earlier Pelusium), water was supplied by boat from further inland; in this case the extra effort was warranted because the town was a staging post on the well-trodden route to the Levant. For these reasons, large ports were forced to lie inland to ensure a supply of fresh water and the work of Stuart Borsch (Borsch 2000) suggests that in the Islamic period, if not earlier, a type of weir was in use, possibly to retain fresh water during times of low Nile and to prevent salt-water incursion.

With time, as seen in the Rhine delta, there was a reduction in the number of mouths of the Nile. Ancient authors such as Herodotus and Strabo (Jones 1932) corroborate the presence of additional distributary channels. Earlier, we discussed the movement of the delta coast as Nile waters rose then fell in response to melting ice sheets and sedimentation. Stanley and Warne (1994) also revealed a return from saline to fresh-water conditions as the delta coast moved seawards again. Inland from the coast, *gharaghets*, or natural saltpans, formed and these could also be accessed from the delta distributary system and were a source of highly prized salt for trade.

By the Old Kingdom, the outline of the delta was much as it is today with the exception of the north-eastern part, now Lake Manzala, which was still part of the sea (Stanley 1988). For the rest, coastal lagoons were backed by large tracts of marsh. The delta site of Kom el-Hisn was studied by Wenke (1988), who made a detailed examination of the faunal and floral remains. There is abundant evidence at Kom el-Hisn for use of cattle dung as fuel but there are few remains of cattle among the bones collected, which are principally of pigs, sheep and goats. In addition, the fish bones are mainly bodies with few heads found, leading to the conclusion that these were decapitated, preserved fish imported to the site. A picture emerges of a ranch where cattle were reared in pens for export to the capital zone while the herders ate other foods including imported fish. Wenke and his team concluded that in the Old Kingdom, Kom el-Hisn was the site of a cattle ranch of the type that is depicted supplying the capital zone in the Tomb of Ptahhotep, with its scenes of cattle being delivered by men from the delta as well as agricultural activity by delta men who are identifiable by their stiff reed kilts (Figure 10).

From the end of the Old Kingdom until the establishment of the New Kingdom, the lagoons, marshes and saltpans of the delta fell under the control of feudal 'Asiatics' (such as the Hyksos, including peoples from the Levante and the Canaanites) who had strong trading contacts with the Levant and a mixture of Asiatics and Egyptians were settled at Avaris (Tel el-Daba; see Bourriau in Shaw 2000). In the western delta, Libyan people, the Meswesh, occupied the marshes and were in regular conflict with the Egyptian state from 1388 BC. The confrontation led to the creation of defensive fortresses in the area including that of Kom Firin (Spencer 2014) during the Nineteenth Dynasty.

The New Kingdom opened with military campaigns to the north and south that reunited the Egyptian empire, under the Pharaoh. By this time, meandering channels dominated the environment of the Nile Valley and the delta. Trade with the eastern Mediterranean became increasingly important and regulation (and

Figure 10 Drawing after tomb relief of cattle herders arriving at the Old Kingdom tomb of Ptahhotep at Saqqara, west of Memphis.

taxation) of the various mouths of the Nile became of great interest. Memphis, strategically placed where the delta narrows down, was again renewed as the capital and the enormous temple of Ptah laid out by Ramses II in boggy ground between the islands of the garden city of Memphis (Bunbury et al. 2017). John Cooper (2014) has shown that the central distributary of the Nile was a strategically poor place to enter the delta since it was vulnerable to strong winds and the rough water that occurs where the Mediterranean currents intersect those of the outflowing Nile.

In terms of the basic requirements for a thriving human community, these ancients would have been looking for sheltered areas (away from the elements); fresh water (with an abundance of wildlife) and a flat terrain allowing both easy access to trade routes (either by sea or road) and for the development of agricultural practices. The subsidiary mouths proved safer to access and thus important trading towns grew up on these branches, for example Naukratis on the Canopic branch. Work by Manfred Bietak suggests that the earliest ports were located around 30 km inland of the delta coast where marine influence disappeared and where a ready supply of fresh water became available (Bietak 2017). From a navigational perspective, the continued tectonic subsidence of the Manzala lagoon maintained maritime conditions in a sheltered location.

As the mouths of the Nile reduced in number, so did the area of the marshes and the lagoons. In addition, the beach ridge of the north-eastern delta gradually migrated seawards until it approached its current position around 2,000 years ago. Continued subsidence along the faults that border Lake Manzala to the east and west ensured that the lagoon only shrank slowly to its current size.

The process of management of the waterways of the delta has continued to the present day (Takouleu 2019) with interventions that were begun in the 1930s and continued by Nasser in the 1950s. Irrigation programs designed to reclaim the low terraces that surround the edge of the Delta have also extended the area of cultivation into an area that was formerly desert and are visible in historic images on GoogleEarth. The area of the delta is still vulnerable to sea-level rise and recent observations of satellite imagery suggest that the coastline is retreating inland, as a result of sea-level change. The reduction in sediment rebuilding the delta, now that it is impounded in reservoirs like Lake Nasser, also contributes to the reduction in its area.

7 Memphis and the Head of the Delta

As the delta waterways stabilised, starting during the predynastic and continuing until the Old Kingdom the city of Memphis grew up at the point where the distributaries diverged. Studies of the landscape of Memphis by David Jeffreys and Pedro Goncalves (Jeffreys and Tavares 1985) with the Survey of Memphis show how the city adapted through its long history. The city started during the Old Kingdom on the western side of the ruin field and spread eastwards following the retreat of the Nile. Parts of the community were established on a number of river levees in the area. Ana Tavares (Bunbury et al. 2017) proposes, therefore, that Memphis was a 'garden city' with fertile irrigated (and flooded) areas between settlements that were restricted to the higher ground. By the New Kingdom, a broader concept of the landscape emerged and Pedro Goncalves (2019) postulates that a waning channel of the Nile was dissected to create a new site for the Temple of Ptah that could be accessed from harbours to the south and to the north and it was in this swampy marshland between the Memphis islands that Ramses II built his temple complex. It remains a matter of discussion whether the New Kingdom works at Gurob (Shaw 2010 and Yoyotte et al. in press), further south, directing water from the Bahr Yusuf into the Faiyum were, in part, responsible for the emergence of drier land at Memphis.

Ying Qin (2009; Nicholson et al. 2013) shows that a little later, in Ptolemaic times, a new connection to an old channel was excavated to provide a defensive waterway around the city, setting the scene for the siege of Memphis as recorded in the Stele of Piye. In the narrative, the attackers cut out all the watercraft from the 'North Harbour' (Parkinson 1991; Bunbury and Jeffreys 2011) and assembled them into a giant floating siege engine, surprising the defenders by storming the eastern harbour walls at dawn. Westerly channels continued to diminish and the main river to migrate eastwards until, in the Roman Period (Jeffreys 1985), a waterfront wall with nymphaeum was established to the east side of the mounds. To the north-west, perhaps as a result of Delta-head migration, a new centre was emerging at Egyptian Babylon, where a Roman watergate remains today. Memphis waned and fell into ruin although new villages continued to track the Nile as it moved eastwards.

As continued influx of sand to the northern capital reduced its importance, Memphis still remained a key town at the head of the delta. As delta consolidation continued, the site provided excellent grazing to cattle despite loss of its strategic and administrative importance. Over time, control of the area gradually shifted to rulers of other lands. Memphis was not the first or last capital to witness waning fortunes at the hands of the Nile. The dawn of the Middle Kingdom saw the site of Karnak selected for the location of a new temple complex further to the south, a town that would also encounter difficulties with changing landscape due to the rapid climatic oscillations of the New Kingdom.

8 Islands in the Nile

The beginnings of sand encroachment from the Sahara to the Nile Valley happened relatively early on in the historical timeline of ancient Egypt. By the end of the Old Kingdom, wind-blown sand from the Sahara started to drift into the Nile Valley first in the north but gradually settling further and further to the south until by the end of the Middle Kingdom the whole of Egypt was blanketed with sand.

This influx of sand into the Nile Valley and delta started to change the character of the river in the valley. Many more islands and sandbanks were formed and some dune fields encroached upon the Nile silts, particularly to the western side of the valley. The landscape effects of this were three-fold: a more rapid reduction in the amount of marsh downstream in the delta, an increase in sediment in the Nile spawning more sandbanks in the river and, perhaps most interestingly, a rapid migration of the delta head, where the distributaries start to divide, northwards.

The close dependence of populations on the Nile meant that every twist and turn of the channel and its meandering became a matter of importance to the residents. Build your temple on the outer bend of the river and erosion and destruction will result. Conversely, on the inside of the bend, sandbanks constantly accumulate, silting harbours and rendering the river more distant. The best way to hedge your bets was to found your settlement on an island. Study of recent islands and the way in which they are used by farmers or brick-makers, sheds insight on the archaeological remains that we find associated with ancient islands. In general, the lifespan of an island is only around a century, no more than a few generations, and the consistency with which farms and temples are located on these island environments suggest that folk memory of the way that islands behave informed the location of new developments.

The rate of river migration is sometimes enhanced by island formation and capture, as described by David Jeffreys and the Survey of Memphis at Badrasheen (Jeffreys et al. 2000). This study revealed the pace of change of islands and the amenities that they offer to their residents. During the early twentieth century, a sandy island formed in the Nile bed at Badrasheen, east of the ancient ruins of Memphis. The ownership of the new island was immedi-ately disputed, with communities on both sides of the Nile claiming it theirs. However, in due course, the island bonded itself to the west bank and became de facto a part of Badrasheen. During the 1940s, the island had a minor channel, partly blocked to the west with the main Nile flowing east of it. The resultant mud was put to profitable use by the enterprising inhabitants who built a brick works on the minor branch of the channel to the west of the island. The quiet harbour created by the partly blocked waterway was an ideal place to load the bricks, ready for transportation. By the 1970s, the island had lengthened and the minor channel had begun to infill, a process that, by 2000, had been completed with the final phase of the infill consolidated by landfill.

By this mechanism of sequential island formation and capture, the main Nile channel has moved a considerable distance over the past century, around 300 m in this case. A similar example occurs further south at Banana Island, now also no longer an island (Figure 11). Katy Lutley's fastest migration rates (see later section) were for just such a setting – island capture close to a bend in the river.

Archaeological evidence for channel migration and island formation and capture is supplemented by more recent cartographic and pictorial evidence. This type of change was beautifully illustrated by David Roberts (1796–1864) in his 1838 illustrated tour of Egypt and the Holy Land. Roberts painted Luxor Temple from the south-east showing a channel in the forefront. The channel that he painted has now been infilled and used for the construction of the Winter Palace Hotel. In another example, an extensive borehole survey of the Karnak Temples (Bunbury et al. 2008) suggested that similar processes had occurred there.

Much earlier debate has focussed on the rate at which the Nile floodplain rises but it is now clear that this change is relatively small compared to the more

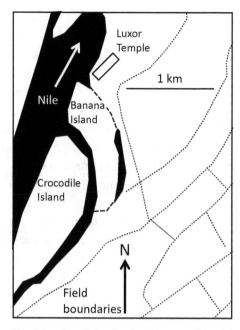

Figure 11 Crocodile Island and the former Banana Island in the Luxor area. The diagram shows the Nile to the west and the fields of the Nile floodplain to the east.

dramatic changes due to migration of the river. Rates of floodplain rise have been calculated by a number of academics at a number of different localities (see Bell 1970 for an overview). Hekekyan's early study at Memphis was ostensibly to work out the rate of vertical aggradation of the Nile floodplain (Jeffreys 2010). From all these sources, an approximate mean rate of aggradation is around 1 m/millennium. The long time span is given to emphasise that the rate is not constant, thus in one year no new sediment may be deposited or a large amount of 10–15 cm may be deposited by one annual flood cycle, depending on the dynamics of the river floodplain. The addition of human detritus raises this rate and in this way many sites have persisted (including Karnak and Memphis) by rising at a greater rate than the surrounding floodplain to form a kom (or tell) and thus ensuring that the community remains dry during the flood season. These koms are sufficiently elevated that many can be seen on digital elevation models (DEM) of the Nile floodplain.

Although the early research was dominated by discussion of the rate of floodplain rise, recent interest has shifted to the lateral migration of the Nile channel. The Nile is a large river set in a sandy, easily eroded bed that rests within a rocky canyon running through the Sahara Desert. As the river rises after rainfall, the water initially accelerates becoming erosive as it picks up and carries larger and larger grains of sediment. Eventually the water, now loaded with sediment, decelerates dropping and distributing the sediment as it flows. As the water in the centre of the channel is fast-flowing, it tends to acquire sediment that it then drops towards the sides of the channel where the current is slower. This process creates levees, elevated banks that are up to 2 m high on the Nile main channel. These levees – broad swells up to 200 m wide – may persist for many hundreds of metres along the length of the river. Levees may also dam the entrances to side wadis or spillways and, after some further floodplain rise, be overtopped to form a lake as was deduced in the New Kingdom case of Abusir (Earl 2010).

Even if the river channel is initially straight, small disturbances in the shape of the channel will grow until the river forms a meandering pattern. In microcosm, the meandering Californian stream in Figure 12 demonstrates these processes at work. The upstream, background bend has a steep erosional bank to the left on the outside of the bend with a series of point bars to the right on the inside of the bend. As the river meanders into the foreground, the water in the channel crosses the riverbed to the outside of the bend to the right which is the erosional bank while point bars form to the left on the inside of the bend. Recent work of Toonen et al. (2017) demonstrates that many

Figure 12 Californian stream that demonstrates the process of meandering.

processes are at work and that we are only just beginning to understand this complex system.

In many cases, (e.g. Mississippi, USA) bends continue to exaggerate until alternate bends meet and a loop is cut off to form an oxbow lake. In Egypt, sinuosity of the river is limited by the relatively difficult-to-erode margins of the Nile canyon (Dufton 2008 and Stölum 1997) and so meander cut-offs are rare. The effect is that bends appear to migrate outwards and downstream until they are 'turned' by the walls of the Nile canyon. In some places, like Middle Egypt, where the floodplain is wide, it may take many thousands of years for the river to cross the floodplain but in others, like Armant near Luxor where the floodplain is restricted in width, this restriction forces the river to remain in one of two possible channels, divided by an island. Where island formation and capture are added to the normal migration of the stream, migration rates of up to 9 km/millennium may be reached, considerably above the normal mean of 2 km millennium (Bunbury et al. 2009).

Slight curves in the channel mean that the current flows asymmetrically and therefore preferentially erodes the outside of any bends that form while depositing sand, as sandbars, on the inside of the bend and within the channel. In many meandering rivers, the classic example being the Mississippi, these meander bends become more and more looped until the narrow neck of land is cut through. Next the channel takes the short way through the cut while the abandoned meander forms an oxbow lake. In the Nile, however, meander bends are common while oxbow lakes are unknown. Meander bends constantly migrate outwards and downstream across the valley. When the bend reaches the edge of the valley, which is difficult to erode, it becomes flattened and eventually a new bend migrating in the opposite direction is formed. Maps of migrating bends made for the Memphis floodplain by Katy Lutley give the impression that they 'bounce' off the canyon walls. Former abandoned levees of the river are seen as low swells in the floodplain and may be preferred as sites for occupation. These relic swells are also a couple of metres high and several hundred metres long.

Katy Lutley, who made one of the first analyses of Nile migration in the Giza/Memphis floodplain, showed that the Nile had migrated over much of the floodplain in the past 5,000 years (Lutley and Bunbury 2008; Bunbury et al. 2009). While complex, the Figure 13 indicates how the Nile can have migrated across the whole floodplain during the period of occupation. Lutley's study was largely theoretical and did not determine the precise position of the Nile in space and time but indicates the type of geometry and migration rates that we should expect for any site in the Nile floodplain. She determined that the general rate of migration is around 2,000 m/millennium with a maximum so far recorded of

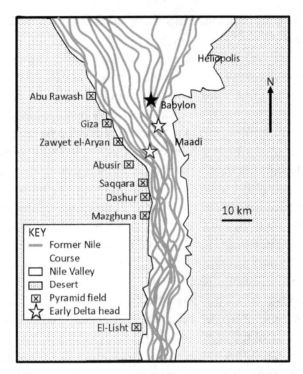

Figure 13 Diagram to show the best-fit migrations of the Nile in the Giza area
over the last 5,000 years (redrawn from Lutley 2007).

9,000 m/millennium where island formation and capture are included. From
these rates of lateral migration, we see that they exceed the rate of vertical
aggradation of 1 m/millennium by three to four orders of magnitude. Thus,
when considering the effect of landscape change on a site, the effect of channel
migration is likely to have been larger than floodplain aggradation. Fortunately,
since there are no tributaries to the Nile in Egypt, the rates of river processes are
roughly consistent throughout the whole of the country, making interpretation
by the archaeologist relatively straightforward.

In some places, the Nile floodplain is up to 10 km wide while in others it
narrows to the width of the Nile channel, such as at Aswan and at Gebel Silsila.
Where the river cuts through rocks like those at Gebel Silsila, there is no
migration while in other wide floodplains, such as at Memphis, migration across
the whole plain is possible. There is an intermediate case where the floodplain is
narrow (< 2 km) and the river channel, which is around 500 m wide, therefore
has little room to migrate. Historically places with this morphology show
persistent settlement and may be strategically important since the river is
constrained to remain near to the community; for example, at Armant where

the Nile appears to flip from one side to the other of a central island (Figure 14). These points are typically strategic since any settlement can guarantee contact with the river regardless of its migration. The example here is around the tomb of the First Intermediate Period nomarch, Ankhtifi. Other examples include Aswan and Asyut, both towns of antiquity that have persisted.

Nile migration of this type seems to have affected many sites in Egypt, including Edfu where the Nile channel has moved across the valley since the area was first inhabited during the predynastic period (Bunbury et al. 2009). In fact, it could be reasonably said that, unless the Nile is known to have been restricted by either bedrock (such as at Gebel Silsila) or monuments and revetment (e.g. Karnak), it should be assumed to have migrated at a mean rate of around 2 km/millennium with up to 9 km/millennium possible. In practice, as the amount of water in the Nile was highly seasonal, until the construction of the Aswan (High) Dam in the late nineteenth century, migration rates were probably rapid during the flood season, Akhet (from July until October), modest during the agricultural season, Perut, that followed the recession of the flood (broadly from November until February) and negligible during the dry season, generally early May to early September.

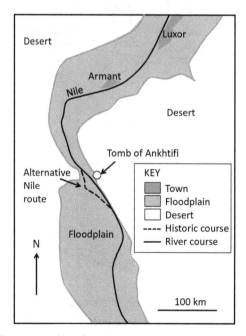

Figure 14 Diagram to show how, at certain points where the Nile canyon narrows, the river is constrained to flow through a relatively narrow gap.

We know from images on the mace-head of the King Scorpion (around 3100 BC), breaching the banks of the water channels with his hoe (Figure 15), that water management was an important function in ancient Egypt. The floodplain could be divided into basins that were irrigated in turn to produce crops and, as is the way of all things, taxes. By the New Kingdom, the extensive taxation records of the Wilbour Papyrus (Antoine 2017) reveal that a variety of types of arable land were recognised, each with a characteristic taxation rate. The basin divides (Gisr), built up to manage the process of irrigation, also acted as roadways that could be kept above the flood level.

Figure 15 Late predynastic king depicted wielding a hoe preparatory to breaching a dyke and thus ceremonially commencing irrigation. Redrawn from the Narmer Mace Head from Nekhen (Hierakonpolis), now in the Ashmolean Museum.

These roadways were often associated with canals and have preserved ancient agricultural topographies since silt, accumulating in the channel, was dredged to raise the roadway. As there was no benefit to moving the basin divide and a great deal of labour entailed, they were seldom moved unless the changes were part of a larger project. More recently, in Graeco-Roman times (300 BC to 800 AD) the half a million documents found at Oxyrhynchus (160 km south of Cairo) and reviewed by Parsons (2007) reveal that the maintenance of reservoir banks and channels was still a major occupation during the dry season. In Middle Egypt, Roman remains – for example, the study of Eva Subias et al. (2013) – suggest that active management of future water courses by excavating pilot channels could be undertaken during this period.

The characteristics of migration are seen in the Abydos area (Figure 16) where islands form on the bends at A and B and can accelerate the process of migration by island capture. Hôd (field-group) boundaries, shown with thin lines, record the passage of the river showing that at C, for example, migration is towards the north-east. The relative solidity of the rocky walls of the canyon means that at C the river is straightened and a bend migrating to the south-west is likely to emerge next. Arrows elsewhere indicated the inferred direction of

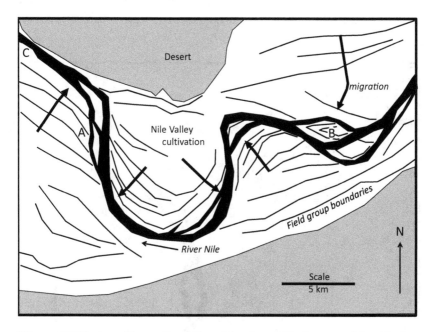

Figure 16 Diagram (drawn from GoogleEarth satellite images of the Abydos area) showing how the Nile River (black) meanders within the Nile Canyon (white area).

river migration at that point. It should be noted particularly that the Nile cannot be said to be generally migrating towards any particular direction but that migration is a product of local topography and morphology.

Our knowledge of the scale, speed, direction and pattern of river migration has improved with the invention and development of technology and exploratory processes. Overlaying satellite imagery with street maps and ancient documentation, provides a picture not only of what is (geographically speaking) but of what was (in historical terms), allowing us to postulate with some accuracy as to how this happened and how quickly. The uses of remote inspection of meandering can be illustrated by a study of Hermopolis (Parcak 2009; Bunbury and Malouta 2012). The Middle Egyptian city, which has Old and Middle Kingdom roots, was said in its foundation myth to have been built upon an island in the Nile around 2100 BC although it is now around 6 km from the main Nile channel (Figure 17). Satellite images revealed that the claim to have been founded on an island is entirely reasonable since mean migration rates would mean that a channel migrating eastwards from Hermopolis would have reached the eastern border of the valley by the time of the foundation of Antinoupolis by Hadrian in 130AD.

Antinoupolis was also founded on the Nile, to the east of Hermopolis, to commemorate the death of Hadrian's lover Antinous who drowned there. Both cities, but principally Hermopolis, are mentioned in papyri, many of which are

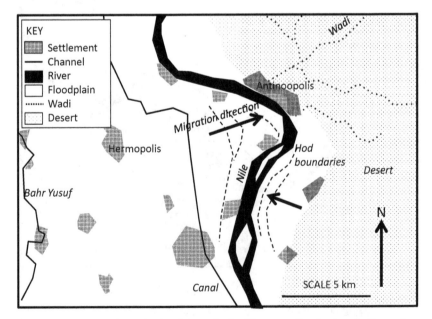

Figure 17 Map to show the landscape in the Hermopolis–Antinoupolis region.

from Oxyrhynchus and the Faiyum and include deeds, accounts and private correspondence. Consideration of the direction of migration from field patterns after its foundation around 2100 BC, eastwards away from Hermopolis suggests that it could have reached the location of Antinoupolis by the time of the foundation of that city. The analysis reveals why documents relating to the recruitment of sailors in the town also refer to their transport to the harbour since the Nile had migrated away from the city by the time of the Roman correspondence (Bunbury and Malouta 2012).

Antinoupolis, a new city adjacent to the desert edge, was at that time undoubtedly in a more accessible position than the ancient city of Hermopolis. However, Antinoupolis was founded with little land since it is located where the Nile abutted the desert edge and Heidel (personal communication) surveys and excavation reveal that many of the monuments were laid out over the desert behind a revetted harbour. The paucity of agricultural land explains why, until the sixth century, many deeds refer to the transfer of land from Hermopolite owners to those from Antinoupolis. The revetments at Antinoupolis mean that the Nile has been unable to migrate away from the city since it was founded. However, the bends to the north and south have started to migrate westwards. Interestingly, deeds from the period after the sixth century tend to be for land transferred from the Antinoupolite population to the Hermopolite one, whose land was, by now, being re-eroded by the Nile.

At Hermopolis, we see how the migration of the Nile across the floodplain influenced the locations of cities and bore upon their relative importance in the landscape. Close inspection of the single large site of Karnak in Luxor shows how, at a smaller scale, river migration and island formation also bear upon the development of an individual site. The temples of Karnak in Luxor were built over a long period starting in the Middle Kingdom and, allowing for continuity of piety, have continued to the present time with the shrine of Sheikh Labeib constructed within the temple. The extent of the temples is seen in the air photograph (Figure 18) taken from the west. In the foreground, the First Pylon dominates the centre of the image with the Sacred Lake formalised by Tutmosis III behind it. The earliest recorded part of the site, known as Tell Karnak and dating to the early First Intermediate period, is close to the top right-hand corner of the lake. The white strip visible nearby is the staging of the Son et Lumiere. Small white specks in the foreground are the visitors and the tomb of Sheikh Labeib, indicating the continuity of piety, can be seen emerging from the trees in the bottom right-hand corner of the image.

Sedimentary evidence from excavations and boreholes across the area of the temples suggests that the earliest Middle Kingdom limestone temple was constructed on an island in the Nile. The temple was supported by a community

Figure 18 Air photograph of the temples of Karnak, Luxor. Photo Angus
Graham.

located on the banks of the then-minor eastern channel (Millet and Masson 2011)
and later connected to the mainland as the channel filled in. An *en echelon* sandbar
was also occupied with a shrine at Opet to the west and the Mut Island to the south
was the location of another settlement. With time, the minor branch of the Nile was
completely filled in and by the late Eighteenth Dynasty (New Kingdom)
Akhenaten could construct his temple (*Gmp-aten*) on the infilled channel. That
temple was later demolished after Tutankhamun's return from Amarna but its
foundations can still be seen in the village to the east of the temple enclosure.
Another temple, 'Redford's Temple C' was also constructed within the new flat
land provided by the infilled channel (Redford, personal communication).

By the Eighteenth Dynasty the northern part of the island had been stabilised,
partly by the addition of rubble to the waterfront, if 10 m of core containing
more than 1,000 sherds is taken as a guide. On this newly consolidated land,
Tutmosis III (Eighteenth Dynasty) constructed his treasury. At the same time,
Hatshepsut and Tutmosis III also developed a new waterfront with a number of
temple courts along the western frontage of the temple. With consolidation of
the southern (Mut) island, a temple was developed there by Hatshepsut
(Eighteenth Dynasty) and eventually the area between the two filled with
sandbanks and a ceremonial way was constructed between the two sets of

temples that can still be seen today. As the land consolidated, new constructions filled the available land and expansion to the west led to the construction of a new waterfront (Figure 19). This waterfront was equipped with a revetted ramp giving access to the river that flowed, at that time, across the foreground. The ancient waterfront wall can be seen to the left of the ramp. With time, the river migrated away from the First Pylon exposing new ground and earlier stonework was then reused to create a more gently sloping ramp/slipway that could connect the temple to the new position of the river.

Migration and further development of the waterfront continued into the Roman Period with the construction of a new set of Ptolemaic baths (Figure 20) on what had been the earlier waterfront (Boraik et al. 2017). The team photographed working in the excavation augered high-energy river sands containing fresh lumps of the sandstone that was used to make the New Kingdom harbour wall indicating that, at the time of its construction, it abutted the river. Later, the Ptolemaic baths, which were constructed over the then-defunct waterfront, are visible in the background, in particular the individual washing cells to the top right of the image. A drain serving the baths is visible to the right of the upper figure cutting through the old New Kingdom wall and passing over later sediment that had accumulated against it.

Figure 19 Mansour Boraik's excavation outside the First Pylon at Karnak in 2008.

Figure 20 Excavation by Salah El-Masekh showing the northwards continuation of the waterfront wall in Figure 19.

Hillier showed that the Nile had receded further from the temple towards the west bank but that the Nile is now migrating eastwards at this point back towards the temple (Hillier et al. 2007). Revetment and erosion management around Luxor means that migration is now very slow through the town. The movements of the Nile around Karnak are summarised in Figure 21.

The distributary channels of the delta also meander, albeit on a smaller scale (see, for example, GoogleEarth at 30° 51' 28.16" N, 30° 46' 40.27" E) and the changes in the Saharan region and in the Nile Valley that we have already discussed also affected the delta. Stabilisation of the river channels gradually propagated through the delta moving coast-wards, a process that was accelerated by the influx of sand between the Old and New Kingdom.

The migrating Nile is a fact of life for those living in the Nile Valley during and since the Old Kingdom and those who lived or made their living near the Nile certainly made the most of the changing landscape. They were enterprising and resourceful, seeking out new opportunities where they could like their twentieth-century counterparts who founded the brickworks at Badrasheen. They also adapted to new ideas and technologies like those to manage the

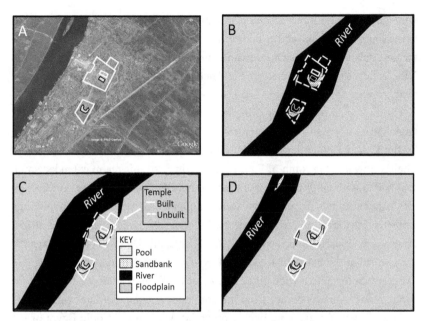

Figure 21 Maps to show how Karnak, now around 500 m from the Nile (A) was initially founded on an island (B) Middle Kingdom temple shown as thick solid lines. As the island extended and consolidated (C) there was further construction during the New Kingdom. With continued Nile migration the river moved away from the complex (D). Pools and the river Nile are shown in black. Key to all fills and lines is shown in B.

water cycles and the seasons. For ancient Egyptians, understanding the factors driving the changing landscape gave them a new confidence to begin to control their habitats; for modern academics, it has helped to place the Nile in the historical context of its surroundings, that of shifts in geographic power and the dawning of a new 'classical age' and a powerful and reunited Egypt.

9 Renewed Strength in the South

During the Middle Kingdom, Thebes began to grow in importance and temples in the area that is now known as Karnak were founded on sandbanks emerging from the Nile. The theme of architecture on islands is prominent in ancient Egypt and a number of important sites have a foundation myth that includes an island. By the New Kingdom, Nile management had reached new peaks and evidence from Karnak, the Faiyum and Memphis illustrate the scope of landscape projects that were envisioned by the state. Climate amelioration during the early New Kingdom ushered in a period of relative stability and prosperity with the Egyptian Empire reaching arguably its greatest extent with connections to the south with Nubia and as far north as the Levant. The return of some rain to the deserts allowed old waterholes and routes to open up in the wadis around the Nile Valley such as the area of the Theban mountain and some more long-distance ones through Kharga and Dakhla.

The first king of the New Kingdom, Ahmose I, from his base at Thebes, launched a campaign to regain control of the delta (Petty 2014) at that time ruled by the Hyksos. When he succeeded, it ushered in a reign that was ruled from Thebes, towards the south of Egypt. The territory of this realm extended south into Nubia with gold-mining operations in northern Sudan. To the north, absolute conquests into the near East were supplemented with treaties with kings further northwards, as far as Hatti, the kingdom of the Hittites (Bryce 2005). Panels at Karnak temple report the later Nineteenth Dynasty victories against the Hittites at the battle of Kadesh Thebes, which testify, although perhaps in exaggerated form, to a wide range of conquests. Further evidence for powerful connections overseas comes from the communities of expatriate workers that came to Egypt, for example linen workers at Akhmin in Middle Egypt or the horse breeders of Thebes who used a specially constructed area along the side of the Birket Habu, a large reservoir, for horse training the imported beasts. Expeditions to the south, to Punt (probably modern Ethiopia) during the time of Hatshepsut and depicted in her mortuary temple at Deir el-Bahri, brought back many valuable goods including myrrh trees, remains of whose roots still survive at the temple (Figure 22). The milder temperatures probably ensured that the myrrh trees and other tropical species could be grown more easily during this period.

By the time of Amenhotep III, large amounts of gold were being won from Nubia (Spence et al. 2009) and used to sweeten relations with kings to the north, including the Mitanni, a people who had a kingdom that spanned modern day south-east Turkey and the northern parts of Iran and Iraq (Moran 1992). The New Kingdom archive of The Amarna Letters (cuneiform texts on clay tablets) contains much correspondence from kingdoms to the North requesting gold among other riches. In Nubia, examination of the extensive mining around the temple of Sesebi (Spence et al. 2009) suggests that conditions in the area were wetter at that time than they are now. There is also some indication, from mining activity in the wadis to the north of the temple, that there was at least seasonal rainfall that could be used in the extraction of the gold by riffling over the natural schist rocks.

Rodrigues (2000) studied fresh-water mussel shells in the nearby Wadi Howar that indicate much wetter conditions there than further to the north where sites such as Giza had already been enclosed by drifting desert sands

THIS TREE WAS BROUGHT
FROM PUNT BY HATSHEPSUT'S
EXPEDITION WHICH IS
DEPICTED ON THE TEMPLE
WALLS

Figure 22 Photo of myrrh roots still remaining at Deir el-Bahri on the West Bank at Thebes (Luxor).

(Bunbury et al. 2009). Similarly, Gebel al-Asr, a little to the north, was not encapsulated by blown sand until after the Middle Kingdom use of the mines and buildings around Quartz Ridge (Shaw et al. 2001). To the east in the Dongola Reach (Welsby 2001) of the Nile, over 450 sites were found, together with clear evidence for palaeo-channels of the Nile, the banks of which were densely settled during the Kerma period (*c.*2500–1500 BC). The demise of these palaeo-channels resulted in a dramatic fall in the population of the region by the first millennium BC (www.sudarchrs.org.uk/fieldwork/fieldwork-northern-dongola-reach/).

By the New Kingdom, techniques in the management of both islands and channels are evident, including the use of the minor channels near islands as harbours and the laying out of new temples within strategically blocked old channels. Chains of islands are common in the bends of the Nile channel, where sediment that has been eroded from elsewhere is re-deposited. Generally, sandbars and islands form close to the bends where the channel profile is asymmetric and the water flows faster and therefore erodes the outside of the bend. As the river enters the straight on the way to the next bend, the channel broadens and becomes symmetric in profile. This spot is known as the 'ferry-point' since it is where it is easiest to cross the river by ferry. Towards the next bend the channel starts to become asymmetric again and sand is deposited as bars on the inside of the bend. This pattern continues through the length of the river.

Small sandbars accrete and consolidate with time, eventually emerging as islands through processes that were studied by Duckworth (2009). The island habitat has a number of advantages. It has easy access to river transport and fresh water, it has freshly deposited rich soils and it is relatively safe from erosion since the channels on either side can transfer water from one to the other without eroding the island. These advantages were evident to ancient inhabitants of the Nile Valley as much as to the modern inhabitants.

Excavations at Luxor Old Garden Site by the SCA (Supreme Council of Antiquities) dig school show that, as the island there accreted and changed, there were adaptations to the way in which the island was occupied. However, the lifespan of an island was probably less than a century, since the minor channel tends to become blocked at one end leaving it stagnant and starved of sediment. Subsequent inundations gradually fill the channel until it becomes a marsh and eventually fills in. Taryn Duckworth's work (2009) helps to illustrate the ways in which islands can be used and why they were so important in ancient Egypt. Islands, being in the middle of the Nile channel were easily accessible to river traffic and provided fresh water. The channel on one side was generally fast flowing while the other, minor channel, was a backwater. These backwaters remain a rich habitat today with reed-beds, fish and birdlife (Figure 23).

Angus Graham (2010) has studied sandbars in detail and finds that, in the Nile, they are generally horned bars. Initially, a sandbank forms and, as the current is decelerated to either side of the sandbank, more sand is deposited to form a horseshoe shaped island. At the upstream end, there is solid ground suitable for a few fields or perhaps a farm building while inside the horseshoe is a swampy area where fish spawn and rich silt is deposited. Agriculture on the island is supported by the fertility of the fresh sediment and the ready access to fresh water. Figure 24, based on studies of the islands of Luxor, shows how agricultural activity and other uses leads to the development and stabilisation of new islands.

In the Luxor reach today, fishermen use light skiffs to explore the inner horseshoe while herdsmen force cattle through the water (Duckworth 2009) to graze on the fresh plants on the island and stir and enhance the sediment with their hooves and their dung. Reeds and other plants that arrive with the cattle, baffle further sediment, increasing the stability of the sandbar until it grows large enough for more substantial buildings and more extensive crop planting during the low season of the Nile. In the days of the flood, additional silt deposited during the inundation prepared the ground for a new crop. A sequence of thin silts at Karnak,

Figure 23 The still backwaters of the Nile rich with biodiversity. There is abundant weed-life, habitat for fish in the shallows which provides food for waterfowl that live in the reed-beds. The palm trees indicate the agricultural Nile floodplain beyond the reed-beds. Photo Rose Collis.

separated by burnt layers, may be indicative of just such a use of the original Karnak island (Bunbury, Graham and Hunter 2008). Alongside the island, the minor channel was an ideal location for domestic activity, landing boats, brewing, baking and no doubt laundering, activities that we know took place at the river's edge from the 'Satire of the Trades' (Lichtheim 1973).

> "The washerman washes on the shore with the crocodile as his neighbour."
> From the 'Satire of the Trades', Tr Lichtheim, 1973

The area around the *son et lumiere* at Karnak, sometimes described as Tell Karnak, appears to show a river levee with steps down to the water, very similar to the stone steps that serve the riverbank in modern times (Millett and Masson 2011). Alongside any island with its attendant domestic activity, the minor channel, although it may be deep, has slow water and is a suitable habitat for large fish. Seining (fishing using nets) for large fish still takes place in these minor channels in the Edfu area and the prevalence of these in the remains from the temple at Nekhen/Hierakonpolis (Friedman 2009; Van Neer et al. 2002, 2009) seems to indicate that the practice has persisted since the Old Kingdom,

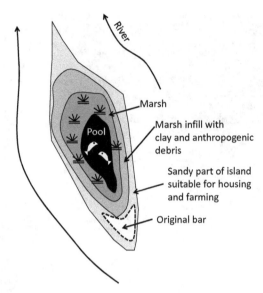

Marsh

Marsh infill with
clay and anthropogenic
debris

Sandy part of island
suitable for housing
and farming

Original bar

Pool

River

Figure 24 Diagram after Duckworth (2009) to show how a sandbank evolves
into a horned bar, then an island and, around a century later becomes bonded to
the riverbank.

when a channel flanked the site. With these combined resources – access to fresh
water, transport and a variety of foodstuffs – islands seem to have been idealised
and many appear in tomb scenes of the rivers of the afterlife, particularly in the
scenes from the Nineteenth Dynasty of the New Kingdom. Heaven was indeed
an island in the Nile.

Evidence from other archaeological island sites suggests that there was
a sophisticated set of strategies involved in managing islands including groins
composed of pots of rubble at Karnak (Ted Brock, personal communication),
retaining walls at the Luxor Old Garden Site (AERA excavation visit) and the
use of low-lying areas for industrial processes – for example brick clamps –
during the dry season resulting in a scatter of slag and other waste materials left
behind. Other examples of island foundation myths and topography include
Hermopolis (Bunbury and Malouta 2012).

Excavations at Karnak suggest that the point where boats landed at the
temples were celebrated at barque shrines, although, as the channels migrated
away, the shrines became more distant from the water and, in the examples at
Karnak, were then incorporated into the temple structure while new barque
shrines were added to the waterfront. For example, the barque shrine of Seti
I was subsequently incorporated into the court of the first pylon at Karnak. No
doubt the opportunity for new display provided by the freshly accreting land
was relished by the extant ruler since the new waterfront could then be

occupied by their monuments. Similarly, waterfront structures such as slip-ways were modified to bring them back to the contemporary waterfront. Dufton (2008) in his work on the koms of the Abydos area postulated that towns had 'rolled' as the river moved. The old town, further from the water as the river migrated, was superseded by new developments along the water-front and as migration continued yet more new developments were made. The old town by this time was falling into disrepair and in a similar example at Naslet es-Saman (near Giza) and at Memphis, the ruined town then became a quarry for stone for the new construction zone. The product of this 'rolling' is a raised area of the floodplain (with few standing monuments) over which the town has passed.

New Kingdom Memphis provides us with an example of an ambitious project to segment a waning channel. By building dykes, Pédro Gonçalves (2019) shows us that low ground left by a waning channel could be used to provide a new temple site for the Ptah Temple. The remains of the channel served as harbours to the north and south. Much of the early evidence was then muted by an even more ambitious Saite (seventh century BC) scheme to develop a large mound at Kom Tuman as the seat of the palace of Apries (Gunn 1927). However, sufficient evidence of the earlier New Kingdom project remains to reconstruct the landscape intervention.

Pédro Gonçalves (2019), in his work analysing the Survey of Memphis cores, has reconstructed the development of this site. He shows how the early settle-ment at Memphis was founded around the shores of an island in the Old Kingdom and developed further during the Middle Kingdom. Manetho, in his history, attributes the founding of Memphis to Menes, one of the earliest kings of the united Egypt. Gonçalves posits that, at times of low Niles, the settlement expanded towards the river but that at times of high Niles it was eroded and forced to retreat. With time, and during the Middle Kingdom, marshy areas became gradually infilled by anthropogenic activity but, by the New Kingdom, more ambitious landscape-management schemes were being planned. These included segmenting the waning channels of the valley to produce an area of reclaimed land between two harbours where the Temple of Ptah at Memphis was constructed. The main Nile continued to migrate towards the east as a series of islands formed and were captured. In common with Karnak, the site con-tinued to develop in the waterfront area while older parts of the city were abandoned and quarried for stone and landfill material.

Memphite monuments explored by the Survey of Memphis and AERA are shown in Figure 24 with the inferred positions of ancient waterways as described by Gonçalves in his interpretation of some 150 exploratory cores from the area. Evidence from fine-grained mud and contemporary New

Kingdom sediments at the same level show that the waning channel was dissected by east–west embankments and the temple laid out on the new low ground. The North Birka (N) and the South Birka (S) remained wet and may have been used as harbours. The map (Figure 25) shows the main ruins of Memphis around the modern village of Mit Rahina. The site is so complex and extensive that the mounds are divided into a number of smaller eminences (Koms) whose names are shown here. The pale shading shows channels extant during the early Middle Kingdom development of the city in the areas around Kom Rabi and Kom Fakhry, while the dark shading shows the formalised waterways of the New Kingdom. Much of western Memphis was later cut down to build the eminence of Kom Tuman by the Saite pharaohs. Not long

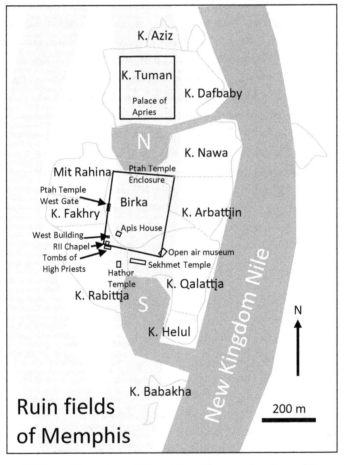

Figure 25 Map of the ruins of Memphis with reconstruction of the ancient channels.

after these developments, Memphis fell into disuse and was replaced by other sites in the Babylon (Old Cairo) area.

Evidence that, at this time, not only was Nile management reaching new levels but that climate amelioration was reopening the desert to travellers, comes from the Theban Mountain, a block of up-faulted limestones, close to Luxor. New arrivals in Egypt are often struck by the sharp boundary between the green of the cultivation and the sandy yellows of the desert. The Theban Mountain in the Luxor area is no exception and today the massif forms a largely barren area, a refuge for jackals and gerbils with almost no groundwater and little vegetation. However, in the New Kingdom, the area became a very busy necropolis with valleys devoted to the burial of kings, queens and nobles, including the Valley of the Kings. During the Nineteenth Dynasty, we know that water was not very abundant in the area from texts found at the settlement of Deir el-Medina. Here they had no access to water themselves and were dependent upon water carriers to supply them as well as sending out the laundry to be washed at the Nile as we learn from the numerous ostraca that were thrown into an enormous pit at the settlement (McDowell 1999). Indeed, the excavation of 'The Great Pit' may have been an ultimately unsuccessful effort to dig a well deep enough to reach the groundwater and its use as a giant rubbish tip was a secondary purpose.

By the New Kingdom, there seems to have been a good understanding, on the part of the inhabitants of the Nile Valley, of how the river and its islands behaved. This working knowledge allowed them to exert a degree of control over the mighty Nile waters, turning what might have been environmental disorder and chaos into meaningful and advantageous habitats, capable of sustaining not only life but livelihoods. The scene was set for even larger and more elaborate river-management schemes from the New Kingdom onwards.

10 High Tides of Empire

Arguably periods of high global temperature promoted the expansion of successful empires, by expanding the Nile floodplain and greening the deserts and their wadi systems. The New Kingdom and the Roman periods, both times of high global temperature, were also times when empires expanded to their maximum extent. They are therefore understandably the periods in which water-management schemes were at their most ambitious.

We already know from the Gurob Harem Palace Project (see gurob.org.uk for details; and Yoyotte et al. in press) that, by the time of Thutmose III in the early New Kingdom, the king could arrange large landscape-scale projects such as the provision of water to some 100 km^2 of the Faiyum basin through a regulator at

Gurob. The Gurob Harem Palace was constructed on the desert edge just to the south of the entrance to the Faiyum Oasis (Figure 26). From the Neolithic to the Old Kingdom (4000–2200 BC) a lake filled the Faiyum basin reaching almost to the 20 m contour. The extent of the much-reduced modern Lake Qarun is shown with dark shading.

The Faiyum Oasis was naturally refreshed during the annual flood as water poured through a spillway that led from the Nile. After the end of the Old Kingdom however, the lake started a punctuated process of drying down to form the rather briny residual lake of Lake Qarun that remains today. Its surface is currently 47 m below sea level and has caused deep scouring of the earlier lake sediments. From the Middle Kingdom, schemes, particularly that of Amnemhat III, were conceived to regreen the oasis. These were succeeded by the New Kingdom project to create a precursor of the Hawara Canal overseen by the palace at Gurob. Boreholes reveal that water was diverted (Figure 27) from the Bahr Yusuf at A into the depression restoring the lake to the 17 m contour (grey shaded area) and commemorated by the construction of colossi at Biahmu.

Recent work with Ian Shaw at the Gurob Harem Palace Project and including a range of cores drilled by Ellie Hughes (Shaw 2010) shows that there was a New Kingdom channel that was dug along the base of the desert scarp, rounded the corner at Lahun and fed into the oasis. No doubt the mud excavated from the channel was a useful contribution to the construction of an impressive palace from which the water could be controlled. Earlier excavators including Petrie and Brunton and Engelbach (1927) described a strong building that they tentatively identified as a 'fort'. The fort, which is surrounded by an industrial area from which kilns have been excavated by

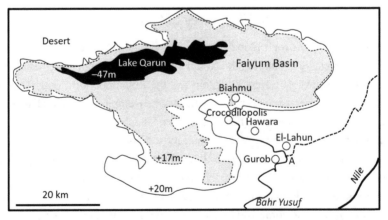

Figure 26 Contour map of the Faiyum Basin after Gasperini (2010).

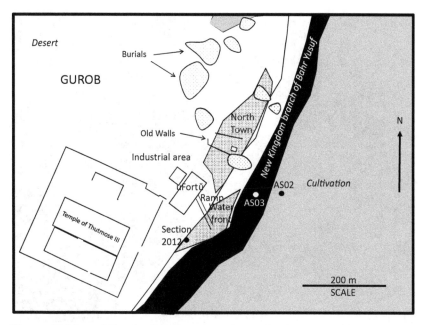

Figure 27 Map of Gurob after Brunton and Engelbach 1927 and incorporating the work of the Gurob Harem Palace Project (unpublished Supreme Council of Antiquities (SCA) reports).

Anna Hodgkinson (Shaw 2010), may be more of an administrative centre than a defensive structure. A ramp leads from the fort down to a landing area (Figure 26).

Satellite image analysis by Sarah Parcak (2009; and BBC Lost Cities documentary) showed that there were other possible buildings to the north of the fort (North Town). Today, erosion has flattened the topography of the site and only a thin veneer from the base of the mud-brick walls remains of these northern constructions but the prevalence of 'lady-on-a-bed' clay figurines, perhaps votive, that have been catalogued by Jan Picton, suggest that the inhabitants shared the normal domestic concerns of the period. Recent excavations by Anna Kathrin Hodgkinson and Dan Boatright (2009 and 2010) in the area near magnetic anomalies show that there were kilns and other industrial activity near to the fort (Figure 28) further strengthening the impression of a burgeoning elite community at the palace. Although the site today has an aspect of almost unparalleled bleakness, our reconstructions suggest that at different times, the settlement was composed of the palace and the fort (Marine Yoyotte, personal communication) served by an adjacent channel, the Bahr Yusuf. The town continued to develop during the Nineteenth Dynasty of the New Kingdom and also into the Ptolemaic Period.

Figure 28 Excavation of kilns in the area of the 'fort' by Anna Kathrin Hodgkinson (Hodgkinson and Boatright 2009 and 2010).

In the south in Thebes (Luxor) we see landscape design in the work of Amenhotep III who, from the Theban Landscape and Waterscapes Project (Graham et al. 2015), seems to have brought a channel to his reservoir of Birket Habu, alongside the palace at Malqata to continue in front of his memorial temple. The Birket has an area of around 2 km^2 and lies at the western edge of the floodplain. The basin required the excavation of a large amount of sediment and may have been an extension of an earlier natural basin (Aude Grazer-Ohara 2012). Unfortunately, its original purpose is obscure although the scale of this and some other similar earthworks to the east, of less certain age, is indisputable. It is notable however, that the basin of Birket Habu captures two of the streams that flow from the wadis into the Nile Valley at this point, indicating that they were likely to have been active at that time.

An additional birket to the east may have had a similar channel to attach it to the Nile and the provision of quays at the temples of Medamud and Tod suggest that they also were provided with access channels. These projects demonstrate a clear understanding of how mud excavated from supply channels could be used to provide embankments or mud-brick for palaces as part of a civil engineering project. Or similarly how, with the excavation of Birket Habu, a raised area could be created to house the settlement and to provide an artificial plateau and mounds. These elevations were suitable for horse training and viewing equestrian contests as well as festival flotillas on the lake.

The subsequent attempt by Akhenaten to establish a completely new city at Amarna on a patch of desert (Kemp 1989), may have reflected excessive ambition on the part of Akhenaten. It may equally reveal an unexpected change back to dryer conditions that rendered the site unworkable soon after it was constructed. The Nile is now around 300 m away from what appears to have been the original waterfront. During the Ramesside (Nineteenth Dynasty of the New Kingdom) Period and after the return to Thebes, many of these earlier Eighteenth Dynasty schemes were taken up and renewed.

Ambitious projects during the Ptolemaic Period include a link from the Pelusiac branch of the Nile excavated towards the Red Sea, later re-excavated after the Roman annexation of Egypt, to join the Nile and the Eastern Mediterranean to the Red Sea via the Bitter Lakes. The next peak of global temperature dates to the Roman Period which began in Egypt in 30 AD. The grain-producing potential of Egypt was exploited as it had earlier been during the New Kingdom. Grain harvests were taxed and during the flood season large grain barges travelled northwards, accumulating grain to supply Alexandria as well as the capital of the Roman Empire. Luxury products from the region included wine which was said to be of high quality.

While the main channel of the Nile remained difficult to manage, the minor channels could now be controlled and having less water and lower velocities meandered on a much smaller scale than the main river. During Ptolemaic and Roman times this manageability was developed and exploited. The Bahr Yusuf, the minor western branch of the Nile, was an ideal partner to the development of a town and, from the example of Oxyrhynchus, a sophisticated pattern of location within the landscape and symbiosis with it emerges. As we have seen from the New Kingdom examples of Karnak and Memphis, sites in the Nile Valley were vulnerable to alienation from the Nile channel, during migration. From Ptolemaic times a new approach was developed. The solution was to build in the desert and bring the river to the site. These techniques, first developed on the more manageable Bahr Yusuf were eventually developed during Roman times to include the main Nile (see also Hermopolis).

At Oxyrhynchus (Subias et al. 2013), the minor channel of the Nile, the Bahr Yusuf, was diverted to the desert edge where the town was founded. Physical remains of the Roman town are visible but more exceptionally its enormous archive of rubbish, dumped in the desert also survived. From these documents, we learn of lovers' tiffs, a kind gift of a puppy to a lonely bride now far from home and many more mundane matters pertinent to the running of the town (Parsons 2007). The combined record of the archaeology and the documents shows that a leat (gently sloping channel), taken from the Bahr Yusuf upstream where it joined the desert edge, brought water to a large tank at the upper, desert edge of the town. From here, a grid of channels served the town in all but the lowest part of the river's annual cycle. The channels brought fresh water into the houses and delivered the used water to the river below the town where there was a waterfront wall. At times when the water was exhausted, a man was employed to raise water to the town and we learn from his correspondence that in a particularly long dry season he felt disgruntled. A downstream embankment probably also provided a nutrient-rich marsh.

In Middle Egypt, the floodplain is wide enough to have preserved traces of much past activity, a strategy emerged of digging cross ditches between sets of levees associated with abandoned channels and minor channels like the Bahr Yusuf (Subias et al. 2013). Most of these abandoned channels flow broadly north–south so relatively short cross-links between them could be dug to bring water to new areas or to turn an abandoned channel into a reservoir. Arguably, it was the Romans who had finally attained mastery of the Nile.

To the north in the delta, the defensive capabilities of the waterways were exploited at sites like Kom Firin. The site in the west of the delta along a now-extinct branch of the delta distributary system was long-lived. It formed part of a chain of sites, located on mounds that flank an ancient waterway close to the modern Firiniya Canal (Spencer 2007, 2014). Delta towns were frequently menaced by marauders from the west and Kom Firin's location on an island surrounded by channels made it a good defensive position.

The core of the site was a relict Pleistocene gezireh at the western end of which a settlement mound (kom) accumulated. Burials from the Middle Kingdom and Second Intermediate Period (SIP) nearby suggest that there was earlier settlement but the town burgeoned during the Nineteenth Dynasty of the New Kingdom. An imposing Ramesside temple and enclosure were built on the south-eastern part of the mound to protect against invasion. Settlement continued around the flanks of the site, which borehole surveys in the local fields show was surrounded by water for much of the year (Hughes 2007; Bunbury et al. 2014). Even though it was a defensive settlement, no moat was required since there was natural protection of the islands by water. Kom Firin continued to be inhabited for the next 1,500 years during which there were periods of growth and revival.

After a period of political uncertainty, Psamtek I reunified Egypt under the nearby capital of Sais and Kom Firin experienced a renaissance. By this time, the northern branch of the waterway that had formerly enclosed the site seemed to have dwindled and the new enclosure was laid out on a much grander scale expanding well beyond the earlier Ramesside enclosure that nestled in the southeast corner of the new enclosure. The evidence from a steep scarp to the south of the site and a relict lake along this front suggest that the settlement was still served by a waterway to the south for much of the year. Spencer (2014) concludes that at this time the community had grown from a frontier village to an established population of some tens of thousands who had limited connections to the nearby Greek trading emporion at Naukratis.

The town continued to thrive during Ptolemaic and Roman times and pottery has been reported from the site continuing until the Arab Conquest. During this period, the dwindling waterways of the delta meant that the site became less attractive. Since the site was extensively mined for sebakh, the paucity later stonework and architecture can be attributed to the exposure of the latest periods of occupation to upcycling, particularly the production of lime and sebakh for fertiliser.

The management of the Nile's resources and effective irrigation of flood-basins required co-ordination of groups of people up and down the Nile. Textual evidence suggests that the functions were co-ordinated by priests on behalf of the king, whose responsibility was to maintain 'maat' (the balance of things) and keep out the forces of chaos. The many texts from the walls of Edfu temple were beautifully preserved by the occupation mound that grew over it and later revealed by the early twentieth-century excavators (see Moeller 2010, for more detail). One religious journey to the Ptolemaic temple of Edfu, described in the texts, is reminiscent of similar, independently conceived pilgrimages to manage water distribution like those of the Balinese water temples (Lansing 2007).

Horus of Edfu was host to an annual visit of the goddess Hathor who travelled upsteam from Dendara to Edfu in the south. The feast was placed in the middle of the agricultural season (Blackman and Fairman 1942) towards the end of the second month of Peret, after the planting and as the early growing season proceeded. As the goddess travelled upstream, her retinue was augmented by representatives of towns along the Nile until the flotilla arrived at Edfu. By the time it arrived at Edfu, the assembly would have included representatives from five successive nomes (ancient provinces).

At Edfu, the goddess Hathor was closeted with the god Horus while the retinue feasted and participated in religious drama. The scenes enacted celebrated the triumph of Horus over his enemy Seth (the desert god). First actors representing the demons and other enemies of Maat, the divine order of things, attempted to approach the temple by boat but were repelled by Horus and his supporters. The drama culminated with the dismemberment of Seth, apparently in the form of a hippopotamus modelled from bread (Blackman and Fairman 1942), and ensured that the next season of inundation could be as successful as the current one had been. Blackman and Fairman also suggest that the extensive renditions of the dramatic texts, accompanied by lists of props and dialogue were intended to continue the good work of maintaining order even should the physical ritual cease.

During the New Kingdom, understanding of the Nile and management of it had developed but the sheer extent and complexity of tributary management during the Roman occupation enabled unprecedented growth and development of the empire. Roman technology maximised Egypt's capabilities commercially in the form of mineral trade and mining, and settlement expansion throughout previously uninhabitable lands. The milder climate allowed city dwellers to flourish because of previously unavailable produce and an abundance of grains, shipped up on barges whilst farmers benefited from new markets. The Eastern Mediterranean formed one marketplace of which Egypt formed an important part. The development of new irrigation and water distribution strategies coupled with a beneficent climate brought the Nile to heel.

11 Coptic-Islamic Times

Roman innovations in management of the Nile established the patterns which persisted until the twentieth century. The ebb and flow of empires, Byzantine, Arab and Muslim, saw continued migration of the Nile accompanied by gentle rising of the floodplain.

Coptic Cairo is an excellent illustration of the interplay of floodplain rise and river migration. Early churches in the area, founded in the third to fourth century are now far below the surrounding ground level. In another example, the 'Hanging Church' of St George was built over the bastions of an existing Roman watergate in the third to fourth century. Those original Roman Bastions are now far below ground level and visitors must descend steps to go down from the modern floodplain level to the ancient one (Figure 29; and Sheehan 2015). FIgure 29 shows how St Barbara's Church in Cairo is now somewhat below ground level and must be reached by steps from a street level that is itself below the level of the surrounding landscape. The approximate rate of rise of around 1 m/millennium is clearly visible in the rising floor levels of successive foundations. Coptic Cairo and the adjacent Fustat, the first capital under Muslim rule which formed the early part of the Islamic city, were originally on the Nile bank and incorporated quays but have now, as a result of migration westwards, been left 500 m from the bank.

Nilometer records that had been kept so faithfully elsewhere began to be kept on the island of Roda in Cairo where the nilometer (Figure 30) is famous for having records going back to the eighth century. Water entered from the river through the archway into the nilometer chamber. The chamber was furnished

Figure 29 Entrance to St Barbara's church in Coptic Cairo.

Figure 30 Roda Nilometer, Cairo from the Nile.

with steps for access and a central calibrated pillar from which the flood-level rise could be monitored. Although it has suffered damage during this period and been renovated many times, the original nilometer is thought to have been built in around 715 AD (www.waterhistory.org/histories/cairo/). Cairo itself has had many centres and Mark Lehner proposes that we should rather think of the Cairo area as a 'Capital Zone' with migrating centres that were, in part, dependent upon the location of the Nile within the valley. Early construction seems to be mainly in the Saqqara and Giza areas in the Old Kingdom when we infer that the Nile or at least a western branch of it was towards that side of the valley. The easterly site of Heliopolis was also at that time on a branch of the Nile and from this Pryer (2011) has proposed that the delta head, where the branching of the Nile began, was further to the south than it is now.

From the Thirteenth Dynasty (*c.*1800–1650 BC) the delta came under new management, that of the Hyksos (rulers of foreign lands) who by the Fifteenth Dynasty had largely taken control of the area. The emergence of the southern capital, Thebes, during the Middle and New Kingdom resulted in a power struggle for the delta, which was finally 're-Egyptianised' during the early Eighteenth Dynasty. This conquest was accompanied by the construction of fortifications such as those at Kom Firin (Spencer 2007, 2014) on one of the geziereh (turtle-backs). Although the channels and the areas between the turtle-backs continued to dry out, the locations of former channels were still visible in maps from the chains of swampy land and minor lakes that marked their former progress until the late nineteenth century. During the period of Mohammad Ali, canals were cut to drain the swamps and regulate the flow of water for irrigation and the earlier pattern of channels was over-written. A second period of water management began in more contemporary times, e.g. during the leadership of Nasser.

Burgeoning trade with the eastern Mediterranean during the New Kingdom had led to the development of ports along the delta fringes and these links continued into the Coptic and Islamic period. Suitable port locations relied upon a supply of fresh water, some of which may have been delivered from a source further upstream and good access to seaward routes and inland connections through the waterways of the delta. John Cooper's (2014) study presents a fascinating insight into the Nile as a working, dynamic river, charting its importance during the Islamic period for cultural, navigational and trade pur-poses. Tinnis, an important textile production and trading port, was said to have become an island during the earthquake of 365 AD (Gascoigne 2007) and continued to be used until the thirteenth century AD. Exploratory borehole work by Ben Pennington suggests that Tinnis was founded on a number of shelly ridges, produced by longshore drift eastwards along the coast of Egypt.

When Atilla (1954) bored in this area, he reported muds containing cockle shells supporting this hypothesis. Longshore drift distributed sediment from the Damietta branch of the Nile across the mouth of the lagoon enclosing the marine cockle spits and the city of Tinnis sprang from the archipelago. The principal sailing season was during the summer when the weather was stable (Tammuz 2005) and the floodwaters were higher, filling the lagoon.

Trade goods were produced during the Mamluk period across Egypt and, at times, made use of extensive irrigation works to produce the crops desired. Agricultural basins of this type occur at Shutb, just south of Asyut and at Akhmin, both well known for their textiles. At Asyut, to form the Zinnar Basin, a system of dykes was created to control irrigation of an area around 150 km². The crops grown in this area are unrecorded but the investment in creating the dykes included up to two hundred oxen and many men labouring to create a lightly baked brick double wall with an earth filling. The importance of the indigo trade at this time (Balfour-Paul 2016) and the importance of the export of blue-dyed cloth from Asuyt to central Africa at that time suggest that a species of tropical indigo was part of the purpose of the irrigation. Augering in the area of Shutb (ancient Shas-Hotep) within the basin revealed that around three and a half metres of sediment had accumulated during the period of intense agriculture, a rate that exceeds the normal rates of accumulation. The provisions for maintaining the Mamluk wall included its maintenance and defence, a further indication of the value of the crop.

Further to the north, the changing geometry of the river meant that what is now southern Cairo became more suitable for the pre-eminent settlement in the area than the earlier sites of the capital further to the south-west, including Memphis.

In the annual cycle as well as longer cycles, there emerge a number of phases: flooding, greening, harvesting and desiccation. From the earliest unification of Egypt, the annual cycle was well understood. This knowledge formed the basis for the Coptic calendar and was closely monitored by the Egyptian state using nilometers. As described earlier, the calendar was divided into three seasons: Akhet (June-September), Peret (October to February) and Shemu (March to May). In the first phase, Akhet, the river started to rise in the south and the flood travelled north over the following weeks. As the river rose, levees were strategically breached to irrigate flood-basins and the inhabitants were forced to retreat to high ground including the flanking terraces of the Nile Valley, river levees and, in the delta, among the ancient *gezireh* (islands). A flood too low was disastrous and resulted in famine while one too high caused widespread disruption of irrigation networks and dwellings. Prayers were directed towards a rise of sixteen cubits, neither too little nor too much, and taxes were set accordingly. Ancient accounts tell of the flooding of Karnak temple and Roman papyri from Oxyrhynchus (Parsons 2007) describe the emergency measures used when an embankment was accidentally breached, including men and furniture pressing into the gap while earth could be recruited to stem the flow.

As *kemet*, the fertile soil that gives rise to the name 'the Black Land' as the ancient Egyptians knew it, emerged once again from the floodwaters, the agricultural season, Shemu, began. Although in the oases a local supply of artesian water meant that there could be year-round agriculture, in general in the Nile Valley there was a relatively short growing and harvesting season; as the land dried out, the season of preparation began. Again, we know from Roman accounts (Parsons 2007) of duties shirked, that a labour tax was exacted from each able-bodied member of the community so that the cleaning, digging of ditches and repair of embankments could be completed before the flood-waters rose and the cycle began again. Indeed, to garner sufficient food in anticipation of the inactivity of the flood season, it was crucial to improve irrigation and productivity as far as possible. Since grain was the main currency, bread and beer being the standard payment from the Old Kingdom (2686–2160 BC) and raised revenue through taxation, the state invested a good deal in the expansion of irrigation. Juan Carlos Garcea Moreno (personal communication) suggests from the records that marginal marshes and swamps were an important source of fish, fowl and game – an alternative larder upon which the population drew more heavily when state intervention was weaker.

In antiquity, the involvement of a network of priests and scholars who assisted the king in monitoring and measuring the Nile and its behaviour through the annual cycle was essential to life in the Nile Valley. It wasn't simply the living who engaged in the taming of this extraordinary river, the ancients called upon the highest power they could – the Gods – to help them. It's clear that mythical narratives involving the Nile played an important role in its management and control. The ancient Egyptians hoped that the Gods would support them in their battle to survive and thrive in the floodplains. The stories also ensured that knowledge of the cycles of the Nile would be passed through the generations, creating an enduring and practical guide to life on the banks of the Nile and in the delta for future populations to use and build upon.

Bibliography

Adams, B., 1995. *Ancient Nekhen: Garstang in the City of Hierakonpolis*. Egyptian Studies Association Publication No 3. Whitstable, UK: SIA Publishing.

Alexanian, N., Bebermeier, W., and Blaschta, N., 2018. The Discovery of the Lower Causeway of the Bent Pyramid and the Reconstruction of the Ancient Landscape at Daschur (Egypt). In *Landscape Archaeology: Egypt and the Mediterranean World*, eds. Tristant, Y., and Ghilardi, M., Bibliothèque d'étude vol. 169, Institut Français d'Archéologie Orientale: Cairo, pp. 7–18.

Antoine, J.-C., 2017. Modelling the Nile Agricultural Floodplain in Eleventh and Tenth Century B.C. Middle Egypt. In *The Nile: Natural and Cultural Landscape in Egypt*, eds., Willems, H., and Dahms, J.-M., Mainzer Historische Kulturwissenschaften 36, Berlin: de Gruyter, pp. 15–52.

Attia, M. I., 1954. *Deposits in the Nile Valley and the Delta*. Cairo: Geological Survey of Egypt.

Baines, J., and Malek, J., 1980. *Cultural Atlas of Ancient Egypt*. New York: Checkmark Books.

Balfour-Paul, J., 2016. *Indigo in the Arab World*. London: Routledge.

Bell, B., 1970. The Oldest Records of the Nile Floods. *The Geographical Journal* 136, 4, 569–73.

Bietak, M., 2017. Harbours and Coastal Military Bases in Egypt in the Second Millennium BC. In *The Nile: Natural and Cultural Landscape in Egypt*, eds., Willems, H., and Dahms, J.-M., Mainzer Historische Kulturwissenschaften 36, Berlin: de Gruyter, pp. 53–70.

Blackman, A. M., and Fairman, H. W., 1942. The Myth of Horus at Edfu: II. C. The Triumph of Horus over His Enemies: A Sacred Drama. *The Journal of Egyptian Archaeology* 28, 32–8.

Bloxham, E., 1998. The Organisation, Exploitation and Transport of Hard Rock from Cephren's Quarry During the Old Kingdom. University College London, unpublished MA thesis.

Boraik, M., Gabolde, L., and Graham, A., 2017. Karnak's Quaysides: Evolution of the Embankments from the Eighteenth Dynasty to the Graeco-Roman Period. In *The Nile: Natural and Cultural Landscape in Egypt*, eds., Willems, H., and Dahms, J.-M., Mainzer Historische Kulturwissenschaften 36, Berlin: de Gruyter, pp. 97–144.

Borsch, S. J., 2000. Nile Floods and the Irrigation System in Fifteenth-Century Egypt. *Mamluk Studies Review* 4, 131–46.

Branton, T., 2008. Development of the Memphite Floodplain from Borehole Data. Cambridge University, unpublished dissertation.

Bristow, C. S., and Drake, N., 2006. Shorelines in the Sahara: Geomorphological Evidence for an Enhanced Monsoon from Palaeolake Megachad. *The Holocene* 16, 6, 901–911.

Brunton, G., and Engelbach, R. E., 1927. Gurob. London: BSAE/ERA.

Bryce, T., 2005. *The Kingdom of the Hittites*. Oxford: Oxford University Press.

Buchet, N., and Midant-Reynes, B., 2007. Le site prédynastique de Kom el-Khilgan (Delta Oriental). Données nouvelles sur les processus d'unification culturelle au IVe millénaire. *BIFAO* 107, 43–70.

Bunbury, J., Hughes, E., and Spencer, N., 2014. Ancient Landscape Reconstruction at Kom Firin. In *Kom Firin II: The Urban Fabric and Landscape*, ed., Spencer, N., British Museum Research Publication 2 (192). London: The British Museum, pp. 11–16.

Bunbury, J. M., and Graham, A., 2008. There's Nothing Boring about a Borehole. *Nekhen News* 20, 22–3.

Bunbury, J. M., Graham, A., and Hunter, M. A., 2008. Stratigraphic Landscape Analysis: Charting the Holocene Movements of the Nile at Karnak through Ancient Egyptian Time. *Geoarchaeology* 23, 351–73.

Bunbury, J. M., Graham, A., and Strutt, K. D., 2009. Kom el-Farahy: A New Kingdom Island in an Evolving Edfu Floodplain. *British Museum Studies in Ancient Egypt and Sudan* 14, 1–23.

Bunbury, J. M., and Jeffreys, D. J., 2011. Real and Literary Landscapes in Ancient Egypt, *Cambridge Archaeological Journal* 21, 1, 65–76.

Bunbury, J. M., Lutley, K., and Graham, A., 2009. *Giza Geomorphological Report in Giza Plateau Mapping Project Seasons 2006–2007 Preliminary Report*. Giza Occasional Papers. Boston, MA: Ancient Egypt Research Associates, pp. 158–65.

Bunbury, J. M., and Malouta, M., 2012. The Geology and Papyrology of Hermopolis and Antinoopolis. In *Landscape Archaeology Conference (LAC2012) Journal for Ancient Studies* Special Volume 3, 119–22.

Bunbury, J., Tavares, A., Pennington, B., and Gonçalves, P., 2017. Development of the Memphite Floodplain. In *The Nile: Natural and Cultural Landscape in Egypt*, eds., Willems, H., and Dahms, J.-M., Mainzer Historische Kulturwissenschaften 36, Berlin: de Gruyter, pp. 71–96.

Butzer, K. W., 1976. *Early Hydraulic Civilization in Egypt: A Study in Cultural Ecology*. Chicago: University of Chicago Press.

Caton-Thompson, G., 1952. *Kharga Oasis in Prehistory*. London: Athlone Press.

Caton-Thompson, G., and Gardner, E. W., 1932. The Prehistoric Geography of Kharga Oasis. *The Geographical Journal* 80, 369–406.

Cooper, J., 2014. *The Mediaeval Nile, Route, Navigation, and Landscape in Islamic Egypt.* Cairo: American University in Cairo.

Dewald, C., tr. Waterfield, R., 1998. *Herodotus: The Histories* [containing Herodotus 440 BCE, The History of Herodotus Book II, paragraph 5]. Oxford: Oxford University Press.

Duckworth, T., 2009. The Development of Islands in the Theban Floodplain. Cambridge University, unpublished dissertation.

Dufton, D., 2008. Meander Bends of the Nile in the Abydos Region. Cambridge University, unpublished dissertation.

Dufton, D., and Branton, T., 2009. Climate Change in Early Egypt. *Egyptian Archaeology* 36, 2–3.

Earl, E., 2010. The Lake of Abusir, Northern Egypt. Cambridge University, unpublished dissertation.

Eiwanger, J., 1992. Merimde-Benisaläme 3: Die Funde der jüngeren Merimdekultur. In Archäologische Veröffentlichungen 47. Mainz: Philipp von Zabern.

El-Sanussi, A., and Jones, M., 1997. A Site of the Maadi Culture Near the Giza Pyramids. *MDAIK* 53, 241–53.

Fairbanks, R. G., 1989. A 17,000 Year Glacio-Eustatic Sea Level Record: Influence of Glacial Melting Rates on the Younger Dryas Event and Deep Ocean Circulation. *Nature* 342, 637–42.

Friedman, R., 2009. Hierakonpolis Locality HK29A: The Predynastic Ceremonial Center Revisited. *Journal of the American Research Center in Egypt* 45, 79–103.

Gascoigne, A. L., 2007. The Water Supply of Tinnis: Public Amenities and Private Investments. In *Cities in the Pre-modern Islamic World: The Urban Impact of Religion, State and Society*, eds., Bennison, A. K., and Gascoigne, A. L., London: Routledge, pp. 161–76.

Gascoigne, A., Cooper, J. P., Fenwick, H. et al., 2020. *The Island City of Tinnis: A Postmortem.* Cairo: Institut Francais D'Archeologie Orientale.

Gasperini, V., 2010. Archaeology and History of the Faiyum in the New Kingdom. University of Bologna, unpublished PhD dissertation. (In Italian.)

Gonçalves, P. M. L., 2019. Landscape and Environmental Changes at Memphis during the Dynastic Period in Egypt, Cambridge University, Doctoral thesis. https://doi.org/10.17863/CAM.35048

Graham, A., 2010. Islands in the Nile: A Geoarchaeological Approach to Settlement Locations in the Egyptian Nile Valley and the Case of Karnak. In *Cities and Urbanism in Ancient Egypt*, eds., Bietak, M., Czerny, E., and Forstner-Müller, I., Denkschriften der Gesamtakadamie, 60. Untersuchungen der Zweigstelle Kairo des Österreichischen Archäologischen Instituts, 35. Vienna: Verlag der Österreichischen Akademie der Wissenschaften, pp. 125–43.

Graham, A., Strutt, K., Toonen, W., et al., 2015. Theban Harbours and Waterscapes Survey, 2015. *Journal of Egyptian Archaeology* 101, 37–49.

Gräzer-Ohara, A., 2012. The Palace of the Mountains on a Re-used Block at Karnak: Amon's *Marou* and/or a Jubilee Complex of Amenhotep III at Malqata. *BIFAO* 112, 191–213. (In French.)

Groube, L., 1996. The Impact of Diseases upon the Emergence of Agriculture. In *Origins and Spread of Agriculture and Pastoralism in Eurasia*, ed., Harris, D. R., London: University College London Press, pp. 101–29.

Gunn, B., 1927. The Stela of Apries at Mitrahina. *ASAE* 27, 211–37.

Hassan, F. A., 1996. Nile Floods and Political Disorder in Early Egypt. In *Third Millennium BC Climate Change and Old World Collapse*, eds., Dalfes, H. N., Kukla, G., and Weiss, H., Berlin: Springer, pp. 1–23.

Hillier, J. K., Bunbury, J. M., and Graham, A., 2007. Monuments on a Migrating Nile, *Journal of Archaeological Science* 34, 1011–15.

Hobbs, J. J., 1990. *Bedouin Life in the Egyptian Wilderness*. Cairo: American University in Cairo Press.

Hodgkinson, A. K., and Boatright, D., 2009. Cleaning the Kiln Areas Previously Excavated by Brunton and Engelbach in Gridsquares N8-9. In *Report to the SCA on Archaeological Survey Undertaken at Medinet el-Gurob*, ed., Shaw, I., 1–22 April, pp. 18–20.

Hodgkinson, A. K., and Boatright, D., 2010. The Kiln Excavation. In *Report to the SCA on Archaeological Survey and Excavation Undertaken at Medinet el-Gurob*, ed., Shaw, I., 4–15 April, pp. 13–16.

Hoffman, M. A., Hamroush, H. A., and Allen, R. O., 1986. The Environmental Evolution of an Early Egyptian Urban Centre: Archaeological and Geochemical Investigations at Hierakonpolis. *Geoarchaeology* 2, 1, 1–3.

Hughes, E., 2007. In Search of the Wild Western Branch of the Nile. Cambridge University, unpublished dissertation.

Jeffreys, D. G., 1985. *The Survey of Memphis I: The Archaeological Report*. London: Egypt Exploration Society.

Jeffreys, D. G., 2010. *The Survey of Memphis VII: The Hekekyan Papers and Other Sources for the Survey of Memphis*. London: Egypt Exploration Society, pp. 5–10.

Jeffreys, D. G., Bourriau, J., and Johnson, W. R., 2000. Memphis 1999, *Journal of Egyptian Archaeology* 86, 1, 5–12.

Jeffreys, D. G., and Tavares, A., 1994. The Historic Landscape of Early Dynastic Memphis. *MDAIK* 50, 143–73.

Jones, H. L., 1932. Strabo, c. 40 BCE. In *Strabo Geography Book 17*, 1:4 Loeb Classical Library, tr. H. L. Jones, eds., Henderson, J., and Goold, G. P., London: Harvard University Press, pp. 13.

Kemp, B., 1989. *Ancient Egypt: Anatomy of a Civilisation*. London: Routledge.

Kröpelin, S., Verschuren, D., Lézine, A.-M., et al., 2008. Climate-Driven Ecosystem Succession in the Sahara: The Past 6000 Years, *Science* 320, 5877, 765–768.

Kuper, R., and Kröpelin, S., 2006. Climate-Controlled Holocene Occupation in the Sahara: Motor of Africa's Evolution, *Science* 313, 803–7.

Lansing, S. J., 2007. *Priests and Programmers: Technologies of Power in the Engineered Landscape of Bali*. Princeton: Princeton University Press.

Lehner, M., 2009. *Capital Zone Walk-about 2006: Spot Heights on the Third Millennium Landscape in Giza Occasional Papers*. Boston, MA: Ancient Egypt Research Associates, pp. 97–151.

Lehner, M., Kamel, M., and Tavares, A., 2009. *Giza Plateau Mapping Project Season 2008. Giza Occasional Papers*. Boston, MA: Ancient Egypt Research Associates, pp. 9–46.

Lichtheim, M., 1973. *Ancient Egyptian Literature: Volume I: The Old and Middle Kingdoms*. London: University of California Press.

Lichtheim, M., 2006. *Ancient Egyptian Literature: Volume III: The Late Period*. Berkeley: University of California Press.

Lutley, C. J., and Bunbury, J. M., 2008. The Nile on the Move, *Egyptian Archaeology* 32, 3–5.

Macklin, M. G., Toonen, W. H. J., Woodward, J. C., et al., 2015. A New Model of River Dynamics, Hydroclimatic Change and Human Settlement in the Nile Valley Derived from Âeta-analysis of the Holocene Fluvial Archive, *Quaternary Science Reviews* 130, 109–23.

Makaske, B., 1998. *Anastomosing Rivers: Forms, Processes and Sediments*, Netherlands Geographical Studies 249. Utrecht: Royal Dutch Geographical Society.

McDowell, A., 1999. *Village Life in Ancient Egypt: Laundry Lists and Love Songs*. Oxford: Oxford University Press.

Millet, M., and Masson, A., 2011. Karnak Settlements. In *UCLA Encyclopedia of Egyptology*, eds., Wendrich, W., Dieleman, J., Frood, E., and Baines, J., Los Angeles: University of California Los Angeles.

Moeller, N., 2005. The First Intermediate Period: A Time of Famine and Climate Change? *Ägypten Und Levante / Egypt and the Levant* 15, 153–67.

Moeller, N., 2010. Tell Edfu: Preliminary Report on Seasons 2005–2009, *Journal of the American Research Center in Egypt* 46, 81–111.

Moran, W. L., 1992. *The Amarna Letters*. Baltimore, MD: Johns Hopkins University Press.

Murray, G. W., 1935. *Sons of Ishmael: A Study of the Egyptian Bedouin*. London: Routledge [reprinted 2012].

Nicholson, P. T., Harrison, J., Ikram, S., Earl, E., and Qin, Y., 2013. Geoarchaeological and Environmental Work at the Sacred Animal Necropolis, North Saqqara, Egypt, *Studia Quaternaria* 30, 83–9.

Parcak, S. H., 2009. *Satellite Remote Sensing for Archaeology*. London: Routledge.

Parkinson, R., 1991. *Voices from Ancient Egypt*. London: British Museum.

Parsons, P., 2007. *City of the Sharp-Nosed Fish: Greek Lives in Roman Egypt*. Chatham, UK: Phoenix.

Pennington, B. T., Bunbury, J. M., and Hovius, N., 2016. Emergence of Civilization, Changes in Fluvio-Deltaic Style, and Nutrient Redistribution Forced by Holocene Sea-Level Rise. *Geoarchaeology* 31, 3, 194–210. http://doi.org/10.1002/gea.21539

Petty, B., 2014. *Ahmose: An Egyptian Soldier's Story*. Littleton, CO: Museum Tours Press.

Phillips, R., Holdaway, S. J., Wendrich, W., and Cappers, R., 2012. Mid-Holocene Occupation of Egypt and Global Climatic Change, *Quaternary International* 251, 64–76.

Pokorny, P., Kocar, P., Suvova, Z., and Bezdek, A., 2009. Palaeoecology of Abusir South According to Plant and Animal Remains. In *Abusir 13. Abusir South 2: Tomb Complex of the Vizier Qar, his Sons Qar Junior and Senedjemib, and Iykai*, ed., Barta, M., Prague: Czech Institute of Egyptology, pp. 29–48.

Pryer, L., 2011. The Landscape of the Egyptian Middle Kingdom Capital Itj-Tawi. Cambridge University, unpublished dissertation.

Qin, Y., 2009. The Development of the Memphite Floodplain, Egypt. Cambridge University, unpublished dissertation.

Quibell, J. E., 1900. *Hierakonpolis I*. Egyptian Research Account 4. London: B. Quaritch. http://archive.org/details/hierakonpolis00greegoog

Ritner, R., and Moeller, N., 2014. The Ahmose 'Tempest Stela', Thera and Comparative Chronology, *Journal of Near Eastern Studies* 73, 1, 1–19.

Rodrigues, D., Abell, P. I., and Kropelin, S., 2000. Seasonality in the Early Holocene Climate of Northwest Sudan: Interpretation of Etheria Elliptica Shell Isotopic Data, *Global and Planetary Change* 26, 181–7.

Rohde, R., 2006. Global Warming Art. For example: www.pinterest.com/mikaidt/climate-change-art

Rowland, J. M., and Tassie, G. J., 2014. Prehistoric Sites along the Edge of the Western Nile Delta: Report on the Results of the Imbaba Prehistoric Survey 2013–14, *Journal of Egyptian Archaeology* 100, 56–71.

Said, R., 1962. *The Geology of Egypt*. Amsterdam: Elsevier.

Said, R., 1981. *The Geological Evolution of the River Nile*. New York: Springer Verlag.

Said, R., 1993. *The River Nile: Geology, Hydrology and Utilization*. Oxford: Pergamon Press.

Sampsell, B. M., 2014 (revised ed.). *The Geology of Egypt: A Traveller's Handbook*. Cairo: American University in Cairo Press.

Shaw, I., ed., 2003. *The Oxford History of Ancient Egypt*. Oxford: Oxford University Press.

Shaw, I., 2010. Report to the SCA on Archaeological Survey Undertaken at Medinet el-Gurob, 4–15 April, pp. 1–17. http://gurob.org.uk/reports/ SCAReport2010.pdf

Shaw, I., Bloxham, E., Bunbury, J. M., Lee, R., Graham, A., and Darnell, D., 2001. Survey and Excavation at the Gebel el-Asr Gneiss and Quartz Quarries in Lower Nubia (1997–2000), *Antiquity* 75, 33–4.

Shaw, I., Bunbury, J., and Jameson, R., 1999. Emerald Mining in Roman and Byzantine Egypt, *Journal of Roman Archaeology* 12, 203–21.

Sheehan, P., 2015. *Babylon of Egypt: The Archaeology of Old Cairo and the Origins of the City*. Cairo: American University in Cairo Press.

Spence, K. E., Rose P., Bunbury J., et al., 2009. Fieldwork at Sesebi 2009. *Sudan and Nubia* 13, 38–47.

Spencer, N., 2007. *Kom Firin I: The Ramesside Temple and the Site Survey*. London: the British Museum.

Spencer, N., 2014. *Kom Firin II: The Urban Fabric and Landscape*. London: The British Museum.

Stanley, D. J., 1988. Subsidence in the North-Eastern Nile Delta: Rapid Rates, Possible Causes, and Consequences, *Science* 240, 4851, 497–500.

Stanley, D. J., and Warne, A. G., 1993. Recent Geological Evolution and Human Impact, *Science* 260, 5108, 628–34.

Stanley, D. J., and Warne, A. G., 1994. Worldwide Initiation of Holocene Marine Deltas by Deceleration of Sea-Level Rise. *Science* 265, 5169, 228–31.

Stanley, J.-D., Krom, M. D., Cliff, R. A., and Woodward, J. C., 2003. Nile Flow Failure at the End of the Old Kingdom, Egypt: Strontium Isotopic and Petrologic Evidence, *Geoarchaeology* 18, 395–402.

Stølum, H.-H., 1997. River Meandering as a Self-Organisation Process. University of Cambridge, unpublished PhD dissertation.

Subias, E., Fiz, I., and Cuesta, R., 2013. The Middle Nile Valley: Elements in an Approach to the Structuring of the Landscape from the Greco-Roman Era to the Nineteenth Century, *Quaternary International* 312, 27–44.

Takouleu, J. M., 2019. Egypt: Government to Launch More Water-Efficient Irrigation System. *Afrik 21*. www.afrik21.africa/en/

Tammuz, O., 2005. Mare Clausum? Sailing Seasons in the Mediterranean in Early Antiquity, *Mediterranean Historical Review* 20, 145–62.

Thompson, J., 2015. *Wonderful Things: A History of Egyptology. 1: From Antiquity to 1881*. Cairo: American University in Cairo Press.

Toonen, W., 2013. *A Holocene Flood Record of the Lower Rhine*. Utrecht University Repository, dissertation. http://igitur-archive.library.uu.nl/disser tations/2013-0923-200637/UUindex.html

Toonen, W., Graham, A., Pennington, B., et al., 2017. Holocene Fluvial History of the Nile's West Bank at Ancient Thebes, Luxor, Egypt and Its Relation with Cultural Dynamics and Basin-Wide Hydroclimatic Variability, *Geoarcaheology* 33, 273–90. https://doi.org/10.1002/gea.21631

Tristant, Y., 2004. L'Habitat Pre-Dynastique de la Vallee du Nil: Vivre sur le rives du Nil aux V et IV Millenaires, Oxford: Archaeopress.

Van Neer, W., Linseele,V., and Friedman, R., 2002. Animal Burials and Food Offerings at the Elite Cemetery HK6 of Hierakonpolis. In *Egypt at Is Origins: Studies in Memory of Barbara Adams*, eds., Hendrickx, S., Friedman, R. F., Cialowicz, K. M., and Chlodnicki, M. Leuven: Peeters.

Van Neer, W., Linseele, V., and Friedman, R., 2009. Special Animals from a Special Place? The Fauna from HK29A at Predynastic Hierakonpolis, *Journal of the American Research Center in Egypt* 45, 105–36.

Verstraeten, G., Mohamed, I., Notebaert, B., and Willems, H., 2017. The Dynamic Nature of the Transition from the Nile Floodplain to the Desert in Central Egypt since the Mid-Holocene. In *The Nile: Natural and Cultural Landscape in Egypt*, eds., Willems, H., and Dahms, J.-M., Mainzer Historische Kulturwissenschaften 36, Berlin: de Gruyter, pp. 239–54.

Weerts, H. 1996. Complex Confining Layers: Architecture and Hydraulic Properties of Holoene and Late Weichselian Deposits in the Fluvial Thine-Meuse Delta. The Netherlands, Utrecht, PhD thesis (*Netherlands Geographical Studies* 213).

Welsby, D. A., 2001. *Life on the Desert Edge: Seven Thousand Years of Settlement in the Northern Dongola Reach, Sudan*. SARS Monograph no. 7, London / BAR Int. Ser. 980, Oxford.

Wendorf, F., and Schild, R., 1998. Nabta Playa and Its Role in Northeastern African Prehistory. *Journal of Anthropological Archaeology* 17, 97–123.

Wenke, R. J., 1988. Kom El-Hisn: Excavation of and Old Kingdom Settlement in the Egyptian Delta. *JARCE* 25, 5–34.

Wilson, P., 2006. *The Survey of Saïs (Sa el-Hagar), 1997–2002: Excavation Memoirs*. Egypt Exploration Society. London: Oxbow Books.

Woodward, J. C., Macklin, M. G., Krom, M. D., and Williams, A. J., 2007. *The Nile: Evolution, Quarternary River Environments and Material Fluxes in Large Rivers, Geomorphology and Management*, ed., Gupta, A., Hoboken, NJ: Wiley, pp. 261–92.

Yoyotte, M., Pillon, A., Darras, L., et al., 2019. Nouvelles recherches sur le site de Gourob, *Bulletin de l'Institut français d'archéologie orientale (BIFAO)*, 118, 555–609.

Acknowledgements

We owe thanks to the many inspectors of antiquities in Egypt who have assisted our work as well as to the ministers and secretaries of the Ministry of Antiquities/ Supreme Council of Antiquities under whose aegis permission was granted. Particular supporters include Mr Mansour Boraik and Mr Suleyman Ibrahim in Luxor. To our colleagues and students, we owe a great debt not only for work shared but also for many discussions of our ideas. The errors of understanding in this Element remain our own.

Our work has continued through the generosity of The Egypt Exploration Society, The British Academy, The British Museum, The Gurob Harem Palace Project, The Friends of Nekhen, Ancient Egypt Research Associates, New Kingdom Research Foundation, Centre National des Récherces Scientifiques, Metropolitan Museum, American University in Cairo and Cambridge University. We are also much indebted to our families for their practical support and to the Farouk family of Luxor who have provided logistical infrastructure and many cups of tea.

Since no book project can continue without the encouragement of its editorial team, I extend our thanks to Edgar Mendez and the reviewers for steering us so deftly through the process.

Cambridge Elements ≡

Ancient Egypt in Context

Gianluca Miniaci
University of Pisa

Gianluca Miniaci is Associate Professor in Egyptology at the University of Pisa, Honorary Researcher at the Institute of Archaeology, UCL – London, and Chercheur associé at the École Pratique des Hautes Études, Paris. He is currently co-director of the archaeological mission at Zawyet Sultan (Menya, Egypt). His main research interest focuses on the social history and the dynamics of material culture in the Middle Bronze Age Egypt and its interconnections between the Levant, Aegean, and Nubia.

Juan Carlos Moreno García
CNRS, Paris

Juan Carlos Moreno García (PhD in Egyptology, 1995) is a CNRS senior researcher at the University of Paris IV-Sorbonne, as well as lecturer on social and economic history of ancient Egypt at the École des Hautes Études en Sciences Sociales (EHESS) in Paris. He has published extensively on the administration, socio-economic history, and landscape organization of ancient Egypt, usually in a comparative perspective with other civilizations of the ancient world, and has organized several conferences on these topics.

Anna Stevens
University of Cambridge and Monash University

Anna Stevens is a research archaeologist with a particular interest in how material culture and urban space can shed light on the lives of the non-elite in ancient Egypt. She is Senior Research Associate at the McDonald Institute for Archaeological Research and Assistant Director of the Amarna Project (both University of Cambridge).

About the Series
The aim of this Elements series is to offer authoritative but accessible overviews of foundational and emerging topics in the study of ancient Egypt, along with comparative analyses, translated into a language comprehensible to non-specialists. Its authors will take a step back and connect ancient Egypt to the world around, bringing ancient Egypt to the attention of the broader humanities community and leading Egyptology in new directions.

Cambridge Elements ☰

Ancient Egypt in Context

Elements in the Series